Kids' Embroidery

Kristin Nicholas

Photographs by John Gruen

STEWART, TABORI & CHANG   NEW YORK

For my dear grandmother Frieda Röessler Nicholas, and for all of the grandmothers who encourage their grandchildren to follow their dreams.

Published in 2004 by
Stewart, Tabori & Chang
115 West 18th Street
New York, NY 10011

Canadian Distribution:
Canadian Manda Group
One Atlantic Avenue, Suite 105
Toronto, Ontario M6K 3E7
Canada

Library of Congress Cataloging-in-Publication Data
is available on record with the Library of Congress.
ISBN: 1-58479-366-x

The text of this book was composed in Sauna designed by Underware

Stewart, Tabori & Chang is a subsidiary of

LA MARTINIÈRE
GROUPE

Edited by Melanie Falick
Designed by Jennifer Wagner
Production by Kim Tyner

Introduction

To embroider means to embellish, or decorate, a piece of fabric with a needle and thread. It's really just fancy sewing. In *Kids' Embroidery* you will discover a lot of ways to have fun. You can work on a grid and do needlepoint or cross-stitch, or you can work in a less structured way and do freeform embroidery, which is a lot like drawing. People have been embroidering all over the world for thousands of years.

This book shows many different types of projects—coasters, journal covers, pincushions, scarves, bags, stuffed animals, and more. Most of them only take a couple of hours to complete. Many of the projects in the photographs were actually stitched by the kids modeling with them. You can start by learning the basic stitches at the beginning of each chapter on scrap fabric or you can jump right into the projects and learn as you go. If you don't want to make the exact projects you see here, make them your own way. For example, use the motif (design) and stitches shown to create something else, such as an embroidered picture to frame, a bookmark, a decoration on a piece of clothing, anything you like.

When you begin embroidering, try not to think about being perfect. As you practice, your stitching will naturally improve. In no time, your stitches will be neat and even. When you look back at your first projects, you will probably love—or at least laugh at—any strange-looking stitches. Amazingly, each time you touch a piece of embroidery you have made, you will probably remember where you were and what was happening in your life at that time.

If you embroider gifts for family members or friends, they are sure to treasure them. There's really nothing like something handmade to show people that you think they're special.

You can embroider almost anywhere—in a car, in the library, at the park, or in your room—for a few minutes or a few hours. You can embroider while you're listening to music, watching television, or even talking with friends.

Now, let's begin! The choices are all yours—the stitches, the colors, the threads, the fabrics. Use this book as a guide but let your creative side loose and explore. And once you learn how to embroider, be sure to teach others so they can have fun with it, too.

Attention Lefties

If you are left-handed and don't feel comfortable making your stitches the way they are shown, then try this: Turn the book upside down so that the stitch illustrations are upside down. Follow the instructions as they are written, but every time the instructions say right, substitute left (and when they say left, substitute right). It may help to photocopy the page of instructions for the stitch you are working on so that you can read the photocopied words of the instructions right-side up while you are looking at the illustrations upside down.

Let's Get Started!

Embroidery is a wonderful craft
that you can learn to do with just a few basic
tools available at most craft stores.
For almost every project, you need fabric, a needle,
pins, embroidery scissors, and a short ruler.
Ideally, you should keep all of these tools in a
special place, such as a basket or small bag.
That way you'll never lose your tools and
they'll always be ready and waiting for you when
you want to start stitching.

Learning Together!

Amie and Kellie embroider
stars in straight stitch for a
Personal Pincushion (page 66).

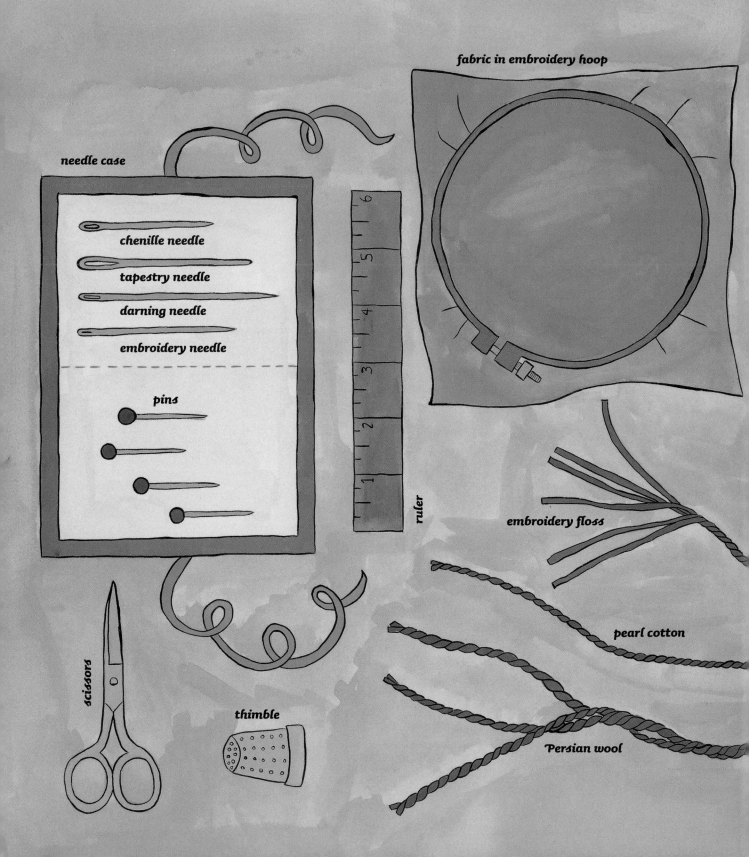

fabric in embroidery hoop

needle case

chenille needle

tapestry needle

darning needle

embroidery needle

pins

ruler

embroidery floss

pearl cotton

scissors

thimble

Persian wool

embroidery tools

embroidery fabric

EMBROIDERY CAN BE WORKED ON ALL SORTS OF FABRIC. THE TYPE OF FABRIC YOU CHOOSE DETERMINES THE LOOK OF THE FINISHED PROJECT.

fabric for needlepoint

The two needlepoint projects in this book call for plastic needlepoint canvas. Plastic canvas looks like a giant tic-tac-toe grid. It is very stiff and can only be used for projects that do not need to bend. Plastic canvas is usually white and is commonly sold in two counts (7 and 10). This means it has about 7 or 10 boxes per inch. It is the easiest fabric to use when you are learning to needlepoint.

fabric for cross-stitch

In this book, you cross-stitch on a cheerful checked fabric called gingham. Gingham is great for learning because you can work your stitches in the checks to make them nice and even.

fabric for freeform embroidery

Freeform embroidery can be worked on just about any fabric, even blue jeans, T-shirts, sweaters, or felt. It is important that the fabric is thick enough so that you can't see through it, so the knots and threads on the back of the work will not be visible from the front. Natural-fiber fabrics like cotton, wool, and linen are easiest to stitch on.

Shop for freeform embroidery fabrics at fabric stores, craft stores, and thrift shops. Or look in your closets at home for old clothes, sheets, or curtains that you might be able to recycle (with your parents' permission). For more about recycling fabric, see page 22.

When you are stitching on fabric that was not specially made for embroidery, it helps to find what is called the straight grain of the fabric. For more about this, see page 10.

straight grain of the fabric

WOVEN FABRICS ARE MADE WITH TWO SETS OF THREADS THAT WEAVE OVER AND UNDER EACH OTHER. ONE SET RUNS FROM SIDE TO SIDE, FROM ONE FINISHED EDGE TO THE OTHER, AND THE OTHER RUNS UP AND DOWN FROM ONE CUT END TO THE OTHER. IN ORDER TO TRIM THE EDGES OF YOUR FABRIC PERFECTLY STRAIGHT, YOU NEED TO CUT EXACTLY ALONG THE LINE OF ONE OF THESE THREADS, WHICH IS CALLED THE STRAIGHT GRAIN OF THE FABRIC.

With gingham, plaid fabric or striped fabric, it is easy to find the straight grain, because you can see the different-colored threads in the fabric running side to side or up and down. If you pick one thread to follow, such as the edge of a line of checks on gingham, you will be following the straight grain. Cut along that line and you will be cutting the fabric perfectly straight.

For solid or print fabrics, it is hard to follow the straight grain along a single thread with your eyes, so you need to follow these two steps:

STEP 1: Start with a square or rectangular piece of fabric a few inches bigger all the way around than it needs to be for your project. On all sides that need to be cut perfectly straight, fray the edge of the fabric into little fringes by pulling off the loose threads. Eventually you will have pulled away enough threads so that the fabric looks like a solid rectangle or square, with threads coming together at a 90-degree angle in the corners you have frayed.

Select one of the horizontal threads about a half-inch below the top thread, and start pulling it out of the fabric to the side. The fabric will begin to pucker. Keep pulling the thread until it is completely removed and you will see what looks like a dotted line of holes across the fabric where the thread was. If the thread breaks while you are pulling, flatten out the puckered fabric and cut along the dotted line until you reach the point where the thread remains, then carefully resume pulling the thread.

STEP 2: Cut along the dotted line, to make an edge that is perfectly on the straight grain of the fabric.

Step 1 *Fray the Edge of the Fabric and Pull Out a Horizontal Thread*

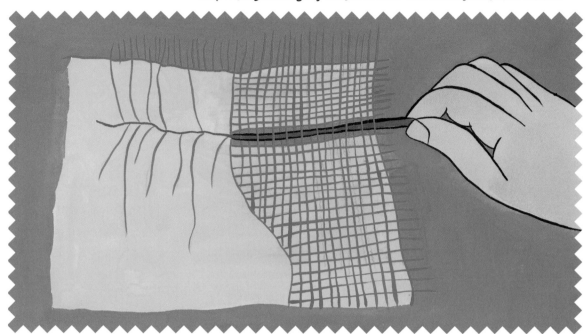

Finding the straight grain of the fabric helps to assure that your pillow, framed picture, or other projects will look perfect when finished. Straight lines of stitches look better when they follow the straight grain, and your edges will be neater and easier to finish if they are straight, instead of wavy with ragged threads.

Step 2 *Cut on the Straight Grain*

11

embroidery thread and yarn

EMBROIDERY CAN BE DONE WITH MANY DIFFERENT KINDS OF THREAD AND YARN. FOLLOWING ARE DESCRIPTIONS OF THE MOST POPULAR CHOICES.

wool

Wool yarn is a good choice when you're just learning how to embroider because its slight fuzziness covers the fabric well, and it has a little bit of stretchiness that accommodates slightly uneven stitches to make them look more uniform. Wool is used for needlepoint on canvas, or for freeform embroidery. The most common kind of wool for embroidery is Persian wool.

persian wool

Persian wool is made of three separate thinner pieces of yarn that stick loosely together side-by-side because the wool is slightly fuzzy. Each of these three pieces is made of two even finer yarns that are tightly twisted together and are called plies, so Persian wool is made up of three 2-ply strands (see illustration on page 8). Persian wool usually is sold in 30-inch-long strands or eight-yard-long skeins (rhymes with "lanes"). Persian wool is made this way so you can use it as it comes, with all three strands held together, or separated into its individual parts so you can work with one, two, three, or more strands (see page 15 to learn how to separate the strands). The more strands worked together, the thicker the stitches. Never separate the fine 2-ply strands because the separate plies are not strong enough for stitching.

cotton

Cotton thread is another good choice for beginners because it glides easily through the fabric. A lot of cotton embroidery thread is prepared by a process called mercerization to make it look as shiny as silk. The two most common kinds of cotton for embroidery are embroidery floss and pearl cotton.

embroidery floss

Embroidery floss is made of six separate strands of thin 2-ply cotton yarn. It can be used as you purchase it, using all 6 strands, or separated so you can use 1, 2, or 3 or

12

more strands for stitching (see page 14 to learn how to separate the strands). Like Persian wool, embroidery floss is not separated into its individual plies because they are not strong enough for stitching. Embroidery floss comes in small skeins of 10 yards each.

pearl cotton

Pearl cotton is another popular type of thread for embroidery that is even shinier than embroidery floss. There are three commonly available sizes: 3, 5, and 8: the higher the number, the thinner the thread.

Pearl cotton covers the base fabric quickly, which makes it a good choice for beginners. It comes in skeins twisted to look like a short rope, and the number of yards varies by size (see page 14 to learn how to untwist a skein and cut the strands). Pearl cotton also comes in small balls, which contain much more thread. Pearl cotton is never separated into individual plies.

Did You Know?

When embroiderers first began decorating their clothes and household items with stitching, they had to work with threads they spun themselves on hand spindles, or sometimes by just rolling fibers between their hands or along their legs. They colored their threads and fabrics with dyes made from natural materials like plants, flowers, and even shellfish and bugs.

other threads

Any kind of yarn, thread, or ribbon can be used for embroidery, cross-stitch, or needlepoint as long as it can be threaded through a needle and pulled through the base fabric. Sometimes embroiderers even use metal threads of silver and gold or silk or linen threads to make very fancy fabrics.

Getting Your Thread Ready

TO KEEP YOUR THREADS FROM GETTING TANGLED UP, IT'S IMPORTANT TO OPEN THE SKEINS AND REMOVE STRANDS IN A PARTICULAR WAY. HERE ARE INSTRUCTIONS FOR EACH TYPE OF THREAD USED IN THE PROJECTS IN THIS BOOK.

persian wool and embroidery floss

Persian wool and embroidery floss each come in a package called a skein with paper bands wrapped around them. The thread is wrapped in a circular formation and the bands hold the circle tight and neat.

To use this kind of wool or floss, first you need to remove a piece from the skein (usually about 30"), then you need to separate it into the number of strands required for your project. (Persian wool has three 2-ply strands and embroidery floss has six, as described on page 12).

STEP 1: To remove a piece of floss or wool from the skein, find its loose, cut end; it will be sticking out the side of one of the loops. Gently pull on the end to release about 30" of thread, then cut it off.

STEP 2: To separate one or more strands, hold the 30-inch length in one hand and, with the other hand, fan the cut ends. Now gently tug on the number of strands you need for your project to remove them from the bundle. Keep the remaining strands neat and organized so they don't get tangled and you can use them later.

pearl cotton

To work with pearl cotton, first remove the paper bands around the skein. Carefully open up the skein and untwist so that it looks like a big loop. There will be a knotted tie keeping the threads together in one spot. Using scissors, cut through the entire skein at the place opposite the knot. You now have a bundle of pieces of cotton thread about 36" long.

To remove one strand, hold the bundle near the knot and pull out only one strand, leaving the rest of the strands held together with the knotted tie around the center.

Step 1 *Pull a Thread from a Skein of Persian Wool or Embroidery Floss*

Step 2 *Separate Strands of Persian Wool or Embroidery Floss for Stitching*

Quick Tip!

When cutting a length of Persian wool or embroidery floss from a skein, be sure to leave about 3" of thread sticking out of the skein so that next time you need thread you will be able to find the end easily.

Cut Pearl Cotton to Release a Strand for Stitching

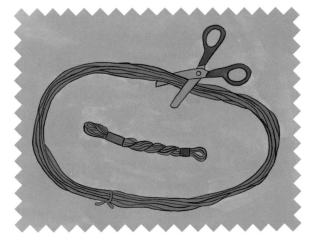

Finding Embroidery Ideas

One of the coolest aspects of embroidery is that you can make almost any design with it—from a simple shape to a fancy picture—but sometimes it's hard to decide where to start. Ideas are all around, if you know where to look.

Ideas from nature

Take a walk with a notebook for jotting down ideas. Pay attention to birds and other animals, the shapes of leaves and flowers, the textures of plants and rocks, the colors in the sky and water, everything around you.

Ideas from books and magazines

Look in books and magazines for decorative borders or fancy type (called fonts) you can trace, or things you might not see on your nature walk—like a lion or an alien. There are books of small designs called clip art that you can get from the library. Each clip art book usually has a theme, like holidays or sports, and you can transfer the designs to fabric for stitching. There are also clip art sites on the Internet, such as www.kidsdomain.com/clip.

Ideas from family life

Think about your family's interests. If you are wild about soccer, embroider a soccer ball on your gym bag. If your mom and dad love ballet, embroider a ballerina on a medallion for them. Or embroider a picture of your pet on a pillow for a couch.

Ideas from doodling

Turn your doodles into artwork. Take a simple shape like a circle or diamond and repeat it over and over to build your own pattern. If you overlap geometric shapes or place small ones inside larger ones, your pattern will become more complex.

needles

WHEN YOU VISIT A CRAFT STORE, YOU MAY BE SURPRISED TO DISCOVER THAT THERE ARE SO MANY DIFFERENT KINDS OF NEEDLES. THE DIRECTIONS IN THIS BOOK TELL YOU WHAT KIND AND SIZE OF NEEDLE YOU NEED FOR EACH PROJECT. WHEN CHOOSING A NEEDLE YOURSELF, REMEMBER IT SHOULD BE SLIGHTLY THICKER THAN THE THREAD YOU WANT TO USE SO IT CAN OPEN A PATH THROUGH THE FABRIC FOR THE THREAD TO FOLLOW. WHEN STARTING OUT, IT IS A GOOD IDEA TO BUY AN ASSORTMENT PACK WITH MANY DIFFERENT SIZES OF THE NEEDLE TYPES LISTED BELOW. THAT WAY, YOU HAVE A GOOD CHANCE OF ALWAYS HAVING THE RIGHT NEEDLE IN YOUR EMBROIDERY KIT. SEE PAGE 18 TO LEARN DIFFERENT WAYS TO THREAD A NEEDLE.

tapestry needles

Tapestry needles have a rounded, blunt tip with a large eye, which makes them easy to thread. Tapestry needles are usually used for needlepoint and cross-stitch because these fabrics already have big holes for stitching.

crewel/embroidery needles

Crewel or general embroidery needles have a very sharp point that passes through any kind of fabric by piercing it and creating a hole for the thread to pass through. They have long eyes for easy threading. They are commonly used for projects made with cotton embroidery floss.

darning needles

Darning needles are the largest of all the needles. They have a sharp tip and a very large eye. They are commonly used with multiple strands of Persian wool on thick fabric.

chenille needles

Chenille needles are larger than embroidery needles. They have a sharp point and a large, oval eye. They are used for many of the freeform embroidery projects in this book.

Threading a Needle

THE TECHNIQUES SHOWN HERE WILL HELP YOU TO THREAD YOUR EMBROIDERY NEEDLE QUICKLY AND EASILY. BEFORE YOU START, WASH YOUR HANDS SO THEY'RE NOT AT ALL STICKY AND CHOOSE A PLACE TO WORK THAT IS BRIGHTLY LIT. FOR THE PROJECTS IN THIS BOOK, YOU'LL GENERALLY WANT TO START WITH A THREAD ABOUT 30" - 36" LONG. ONCE YOU HAVE POKED THE THREAD THROUGH THE EYE OF THE NEEDLE, PULL AT LEAST 6" THROUGH AND DOUBLE IT OVER SO THAT THE THREAD DOESN'T SLIP RIGHT BACK OUT OF THE EYE.

simple threading

For cotton embroidery threads or other smooth, nonfuzzy threads, make a new, clean cut at one end of the thread. Moisten the end in your mouth and flatten with your lips as you pull it out. Hold the thread between your thumb and pointer finger with about $1/4$" to $1/2$" showing beyond your fingers and poke it straight through the eye of the needle.

loop method

This method works well with wool or other fuzzy threads that have little hairs on the surface.

STEP 1: Hold your needle between your thumb and finger with about 1" of the pointy end of the needle showing. Now fold the end of your thread over the needle with about 1" on one side of the needle and the tail dangling on the other side. With the thumb and finger of your other hand, pinch the thread around the needle tightly. Pull the needle out while holding the little loop secure in your other hand.

STEP 2: Push the loop through the eye of the needle and pull the thread through.

using a needle threader

To make threading a needle really easy, use a needle threader. Push the threader's wire diamond through the eye of the needle first. Push the end of your thread through the center of the diamond. Pull the needle threader back through the eye and the thread will follow.

running out of thread

When you have only about 5" or 6" of thread left, it's time to end the thread you're working with and begin a new one. Instructions for ending the old thread are included in each project in this book.

Simple Threading

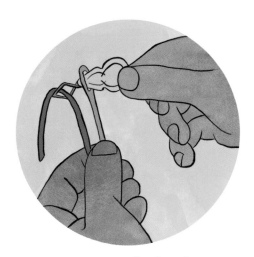

Using a Needle Threader

Step 1

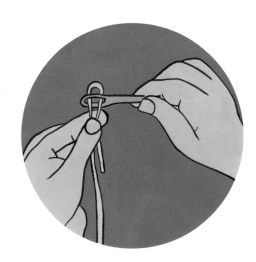

Step 2

other tools

scissors

Ideally, you should have a few different kinds of scissors: a small pair of scissors with a sharp point (sometimes labeled embroidery scissors at the store) for snipping threads and removing mistakes; a large pair of sharp scissors for cutting fabric and yarn only; and an old or very inexpensive pair of scissors for cutting plastic canvas and paper (sometimes labeled craft or all-purpose scissors).

Put a label on your fabric scissors so that you and anyone who might borrow your scissors will remember which ones are for cutting fabric and yarn only. Paper and plastic canvas can dull the blades of your good scissors, making it difficult for them to cut fabric and yarn.

pins and pincushion

The best tool for keeping track of your pins and threaded needles is a pincushion. On page 66 are instructions for making your own. It's not a good idea to leave needles or pins in your work because they could leave a permanent hole in the fabric, or a rust stain if they got wet (not usually a problem if you buy rust-proof pins and needles, but it sometimes happens).

needle case or magnet

To keep track of your embroidery needles, it's useful to keep them in a small fabric needle case or on a magnet designed for this purpose. On page 62 are instructions for making your own needle case. You can also keep your needles stuck in a pincushion.

embroidery hoop

Embroidery hoops hold floppy fabric tight and smooth while you are working, so your stitches stay even and the fabric does not pucker. They can be used for any cross-stitch or freeform embroidery project as long as the fabric fits between the two halves of the hoop. Some fabrics, such as the wool felt used in many of the projects in this book, do not require an embroidery hoop because they are firm enough on their own.

Embroidery hoops are made of two circles of wood or plastic that fit together with a little space between them for the fabric. They come in different diameters so you can work on different-sized areas of your fabric. When you buy an embroidery hoop, make sure it is smaller than the piece of fabric you will be stitching so it can get a good grip on the fabric all around.

ruler and tape measure

Ideally, you should have a 6" ruler, a 12" ruler, and a tape measure. Clear plastic rulers make it easy to see the fabric or design underneath as you use them.

transfer tools

For many of the projects in this book, you will need to draw or transfer a design onto your fabric. Depending on the project, you may use an ordinary pencil, a water-soluble fabric marker, dressmaker's tracing paper, or computer T-shirt transfers. Instructions for using transfer tools are included in the project instructions and on page 71.

masking tape

Sometimes you will want to tape the edges of your fabric so that it doesn't fray or unravel while you are working on your project. If you have a sewing machine, you can zigzag the edges to prevent fraying, instead of using masking tape.

thimble

A thimble looks like a miniature metal cup that you wear on one finger. You can use a thimble to protect the end of your finger when you stitch, and to push hard on the needle to move it through thick or tight fabrics like denim. The thimble is covered with little dimples so that the end of the needle doesn't just slip off the thimble while you're pushing the needle. Thimbles can be plain metal, or very fancy with decorations and painted designs. Some people like to collect thimbles.

needle threader

There are several different kinds of gadgets available to help you to thread a needle. Most have a thin flexible wire formed into a diamond shape at one end. Turn to page 19 to see a needle threader in action.

thread organizer

Craft and needlework stores carry all kinds of thread organizing systems, or you can create your own system at home. For example, you can use a different plastic zip-shut sandwich bag for each color of thread, then clip the bags together with a round ring available at office supply stores (similar to a notebook binder ring), and store them in a cardboard box. You can buy plastic boxes for thread storage that come with small pieces of cardboard to wind threads around. You can also cut $1/2$" holes around the edges of a piece of cardboard, and tie the different colors of your opened thread through the holes.

Recycling and Reinventing Fabric for Embroidery

IT'S OFTEN FUN AND INTERESTING TO EMBROIDER ON RECYCLED FABRIC—THAT MEANS FABRIC THAT WAS ONCE USED FOR A DIFFERENT PURPOSE. FOR EXAMPLE, THE BLANKET-STITCH SCARF (PAGE 98), ORANGE LAZY DAISY TOTE BAG (PAGE 102), AND TEA PARTY (PAGE 134) WERE ALL MADE FROM THE SAME OLD WOOL BLANKET PURCHASED AT A THRIFT STORE, THEN WASHED AND DYED DIFFERENT COLORS.

choosing fabric to recycle

Look for fabrics made out of linen, cotton, wool, and silk as they all make wonderful base fabrics for embroidery. Curtains, blankets, bed sheets, wool coats, denim jeans, tablecloths, towels, and T-shirts can all be transformed into embroidery fabric.

If you are embroidering on a piece of clothing that you still wear, then you probably do not have to do much to prepare it. Brand-new clothing should be washed according to the instructions on the tag.

When you are recycling a used piece of clothing or a household item, examine it to see where the cleanest and best sections are. Avoid areas that are worn, fraying, or stained. Cut out the largest good pieces of fabric, removing any linings, zippers, buttons, and hems, unless you plan on using them as part of your design.

dyeing fabric

If you don't like the color of a piece of fabric, consider dyeing it (with your parents' permission). Fabrics made out of natural fibers, such as cotton, wool, rayon, and silk, dye easily. You can purchase fabric dyes at grocery or craft stores. Look for dyes that say on the package that they will work with your kind of fabric. You can dye fabric in a pot in your kitchen or outside, or even in the washing machine.

Follow the directions on the dye package carefully. If you dye white or light-colored fabric, it will turn the color of your dye, but if you dye fabric that's already colored, the starting color of the fabric will affect the results. For example, if you dye yellow fabric with pink dye, the finished fabric will be orange, the same result you would get if you were mixing paints.

felting fabric

To make wool especially easy to work with, think about felting it before embroidering on it. Felting is a process of shrinking wool fibers to create a thick, soft fabric you can't see through. Most people are familiar with felting by accident, such as when you put a wool sweater in the washing machine and it shrinks down to a size to fit a teddy bear. But when you felt fabric on purpose, the results can be wonderful. Felt is an especially good fabric for embroidery and sewing projects because it can be cut into any shape and the edges do not unravel, so you do not need to finish the edges with hems.

To make your own felt, first get your parents' permission and ask them if they want to supervise. Choose an old wool sweater, blanket, or coat that is at least 80-percent wool, making sure it is not a type of wool called superwash, which has been treated with chemicals so that it won't felt. Set the washing machine for a hot water wash and cold rinse, add a little laundry soap (Ivory works well) and a few old towels, and let the washing machine run on the regular cycle that you use for most clothes (not the wool or delicate cycle). When the cycle is done, remove your fabric from the washing machine and inspect it—it should be thicker and smaller than when it began. If you want it to felt even more, run it through the wash cycle again. When ready, spread the felt out flat on towels and leave it to dry.

Needlepoint

Our embroidery adventure begins with
needlepoint, the easiest form of embroidery.
You start with small coasters and cards, and when you're
ready you can make larger projects like pillows or even
chair seats. Once you get the hang of needlepoint, you may
want to work on projects with fancy scenes like forests full
of trees and animals. When you work needlepoint, you cover
the entire front of the canvas fabric with stitches—none
of the fabric under the stitches shows through.

Traditionally, needlepoint is stitched with wool yarn
because it covers the fabric easily. Needlepoint is usually
done on either a specially treated, stiff fabric called
needlepoint mesh, or on plastic canvas. Sometimes the
needlepoint design is printed directly on the mesh or canvas
for you to stitch like paint-by-number, and sometimes you
need to follow a separate chart. Or you can, of course, make
up your own design as you go along.

An Afternoon Project

Isabelle, Olivia, Celia, and Eliza are all working on Striped Needlepoint Coasters (see page 28).

tent stitch

TENT STITCH IS THE EASIEST STITCH IN NEEDLEPOINT AND IS USED
FOR BOTH PROJECTS IN THIS CHAPTER.

Row 1: To begin stitching, thread your needle and come up at A. Pull the thread through, leaving a tail about 6" long on the back of the work to weave in later. Hold this tail against the back of the canvas as you take the first 3 or 4 stitches so it doesn't pull right through. After you have made a few stitches it will be anchored securely.

Move your needle over and up one space, then insert it at B, and pull through to the back of the canvas, making a short, diagonal stitch that covers one intersection of the canvas. Bring the needle to the front one space below B at C, and pull to the front. Count over one space and up one space again, and insert the needle at D, and pull the thread through to form the second diagonal stitch in the row. Continue across the row, ending at J.

Once you finish your first row, leave the thread at the back of the work after the last stitch, and turn the canvas upside down so the first row of stitches is now at the top. As long as you turn your canvas upside down at the end of each row, you can continue to work all the rows of stitches in the same direction.

Row 2: Insert your needle at K, in the first row of holes below where you left the thread at the end of the previous row. Pull the thread through to the front of the canvas. Count over and up one space again, and insert the needle at L, in the same hole as a stitch from the previous row. Pull the thread through to the back to form the first diagonal stitch in this row. To continue, bring the needle to the front one space below L at M, and pull to the front. Count over and up one space again, and insert the needle at N to form the second diagonal stitch in the row.

Continue across the row in this way until you have completed the second row of stitches.

At the end of the row, leave the thread at the back of the work, and turn your canvas upside down again for the third row of stitching. Insert the needle one space above where you left the thread at the end of the previous row, pull the thread through to the front, and continue as before.

When you needlepoint, it is very important that all of your stitches lean in the same direction so they fit snugly together side-by-side and cover the canvas completely. If the stitches lean in different directions, the fabric may show through where the stitches don't touch each other, and your work will not appear even and neat. When you are learning, it is easier to make sure all the stitches are leaning in the same direction if you stitch in a very orderly manner from one side of the canvas to the other.

needlepoint
coasters

THERE ARE THREE COASTER designs to choose from. The Easy Stripes coaster is the simplest, so it is a good one to start with if you've never done needlepoint before.

(1) prepare the canvas

For each coaster, cut a piece of plastic canvas about 5" square, following the instructions on page 30. Make sure to trim the nibs all the way around so that your thread won't catch on them. This is a bigger area than you will need for stitching; you will trim the extra canvas close to your stitching when you are finished.

tent stitch · whipstitch

Materials

ONE (10$\frac{1}{2}$" X 13$\frac{1}{2}$") PIECE PLASTIC
   NEEDLEPOINT CANVAS IN 7 MESH SIZE
   (this is enough to make 4 coasters)
PERSIAN WOOL (see below)
SIZE 16 TAPESTRY NEEDLE
SCISSORS, FOR CUTTING PLASTIC CANVAS
PIECE OF FELT, ABOUT 4$\frac{1}{2}$" SQUARE, FOR
   COVERING BACK OF COASTER (optional)
FABRIC GLUE, TO ATTACH FELT TO BACK
   OF COASTER (optional)

yarn for easy stripes coaster
3 (8-YARD) SKEINS PERSIAN WOOL, IN 3
   DIFFERENT COLORS (a dark color and a light
   color for the stripes and a third color that
   looks nice with the others for the edge)

yarn for blocks coaster
6 (8-YARD) SKEINS PERSIAN WOOL, IN 6
   DIFFERENT COLORS THAT LOOK NICE TOGETHER

yarn for flower coaster
3 (8-YARD) SKEINS PERSIAN WOOL,
IN 3 DIFFERENT COLORS (a light color for the
   background, a dark color for the flower, and a
   third color that looks nice with both for the
   edge and center of the flower)

Everybody Gets One!

Coasters make great presents for every one—your mom, dad, sister or brother, or favorite teacher—or you might want to make one for yourself to keep beside your bed for a nighttime glass of water.

Cutting Plastic Canvas

Draw the shape of your project on the plastic canvas using a washable marker. Using craft scissors (not the scissors you use to cut fabric or your embroidery scissors), cut the canvas about an inch or more outside the line, one strand of plastic at a time. Each strand will kind of "pop" as you cut it. After the shape has been cut out, go back and snip off the little nibs (points) around the edge of the canvas so that your thread will not catch on them while stitching. Use a little water to remove the washable lines around the edge before stitching. Cutting the canvas bigger than the actual project makes it easier to hold the canvas when stitching close to the edge. When you are finished, you can cut away the extra canvas according to the directions for your project.

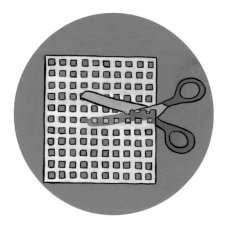

2) *prepare the thread*

For these projects, you need to thread your needle with 4 two-ply strands of Persian wool. Since each skein contains 3 two-ply strands, you need to do some rearranging.

Following the instructions on page 14, cut two 32-inch strands of your first color and lay them on a table. Now, from one of the pieces, separate one strand. Hold the separated strand together with a whole 3-strand piece, and thread all 4 strands on your needle.

Carefully set aside the piece with only 2 strands left, or wrap it around a piece of scrap paper and write on the paper the color number and the number of strands. That way you will know how many strands it has when you want to combine it with more whole pieces to make additional 4-strand lengths.

3) *needlepoint a coaster*

Referring to the instructions that follow and the charts on page 35 as necessary, needlepoint the stripes, blocks, or flower pattern using the tent stitch (see page 26). Remember that each square on the chart represents one stitch. The uncolored squares around the outside edge of the charts are where you will finish the edge of the coaster when the stitching is complete. Leave them unstitched for now.

easy stripes coaster

STRIPE 1: Using the thread and needle prepared in Step 2, bring the thread up to the front through the hole in the lower left corner of the canvas. Pull the thread through, leaving a tail of thread about 6" long on the back of the work to weave in later. Hold this tail against the back of the canvas as you take the first 3 or 4 stitches so it doesn't pull right through. After you have made a few stitches it will be anchored securely.

Work 25 stitches across from left to right. When you get to the end of the row, there will be some leftover canvas beyond it. Just leave this part empty; you will trim it away when you get ready to finish the coaster. Now turn your canvas upside down and work another row of 25 stitches to make the second row of your stripe. Finish off this color of thread by leaving the thread on the back of the canvas after the last stitch, and weaving it behind the other stitches for about $^1/2$", as shown at right. Thread the beginning tail on the needle and weave it under the stitches on the back of the work, too. Trim the ends of both tails to about $^1/4$" long.

Ending the Thread and Weaving in the Ends

When you are finished stitching, or have less than 5" of thread left, bring the thread to the back of the canvas and pull through. Secure the end by weaving it under the stitches on the back of the work for about $^1/2$" as shown.

To finish the tail from where you began stitching, thread the tail on a needle and weave it under the stitches on the back of the work for about $^1/2$", too.

Trim the ends of both tails to $^1/4$" long.

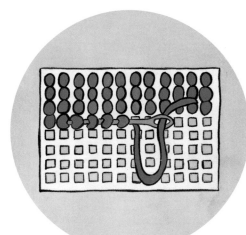

STRIPE 2: Prepare a second 4-strand length of yarn in your other stripe color. Thread 4 strands of the new color on the needle, and bring the thread up to the front through the hole on the left side of the canvas, directly above the second row of the first stripe. Work the second stripe the same as the first, and fasten off the thread.

Continue to make rows of stripes in this manner until your coaster looks like the chart on page 35, with 13 stripes in all, 7 stripes in the first color, and 6 stripes in the second color. Skip to Step 4 on page 34 for finishing directions.

blocks coaster

If you examine the chart for the blocks coaster on page 35, you will see that this design is made of different blocks of color— all 7 stitches wide by 7 stitches high.

BLOCK 1: Using the thread and needle prepared in Step 2, bring the thread up to the front through the hole in the lower left corner of the canvas. Pull the thread through, leaving a tail about 6" long on the back of the work to weave in later. Hold this tail against the back of the canvas as you take the first 3 or 4 stitches so it doesn't pull right through. After you

have made a few stitches it will be anchored securely, and you will weave in the tail later when you are finished stitching.

Work 7 stitches, then turn your work upside down and make another row of 7 stitches next to the first one. Continue until you have finished one block of color 7 stitches wide and 7 stitches high. Finish off this color by leaving the thread on the back of the canvas after the last stitch, and weaving it behind the other stitches for about $1/2$" as shown on page 31. Thread the beginning tail on the needle and weave it under the stitches on the back of the work, too. Trim the ends of both tails to about $1/4$" long.

BLOCK 2: For the next block, choose and prepare another color of yarn, and work as for first block. Continue working blocks until you have a total of 16, arranged 4 across and 4 high. Skip to Step 4 on page 34 for finishing directions.

flower coaster

PETALS: The easiest way to work this design is to first stitch the petal sections of the flower (not the center). Using the thread and needle prepared in Step 2, bring the thread up to the front in a hole 8 holes from the left, and 3 holes up from the bottom, as shown on the chart on page 35. Pull the thread through, leaving a tail about 6" long on the back of the work to weave in later. Hold this tail against the back of the canvas as you take the first 3 or 4 stitches so it doesn't pull right through. After you have made a few stitches it will be anchored securely.

Work the 2 stitches in the first row of the flower chart. Now, turn your work and the chart upside down. You will see that you need 6 stitches in the next row—2 on either side of the stitches you made in the last row and 2 just below the last two stitches. Bring the needle up 2 holes below and 3 holes to the left of where you finished the last stitch, and make a row of 6 stitches. It is OK if the thread travels a little bit across the back of the work to get to the new position, just make sure to pull the thread snugly so all the stitches are even, and there are no loose stitches at the beginning or end of rows. Continue in this manner, turning the canvas and chart upside down every row in order to keep working from left to right. It is OK to carry the flower color across the back of the space you will leave for the center.

When you get to the end of a section, or when there is about 5" of thread left, bring the thread to the back of the canvas. Secure the end by weaving it under the stitches on the back of the work for about $1/2$" as shown on page 31. Thread the beginning tail on the needle and weave it under the stitches on the back of the work for about $1/2$", too. Trim the ends of both tails to $1/4$" long. Prepare and start a new 4-strand length of yarn where you need it and continue until the flower shape is finished.

CENTER OF FLOWER: Prepare a 4-strand length of yarn for the flower center, and stitch the center of the flower in rows, starting and ending the thread as before.

BACKGROUND: Prepare the background color of thread and fill in all around the flower, starting and ending the thread as for the other sections. The colored part of the flower chart is 26 stitches wide and 26 stitches high, not counting the blank squares for the edging. Since your canvas is bigger than this, you will have some leftover canvas beyond the background. Just leave this part empty; you will trim it away when you get ready to finish the coaster.

4 whipstitch coaster edges

Trim your canvas so there is one intersection of plastic all around the stitching. Cut two 3-strand pieces of your edging color 32" long. Hold both pieces together and thread them on a needle, so you will be working the edging with a 6-strand length of yarn; all 6 strands are needed to completely cover the outer edge. To begin stitching, bring the thread up to the front through one of the holes in the middle of the line of holes across the bottom of the coaster. Pull the thread through, leaving a tail about 6" long on the back of the work to weave in later. Hold this tail against the back of the canvas as you take the first 3 or 4 stitches so it doesn't pull right through.

Work in whipstitch all the way around the coaster as shown above. At each corner, you will need to take 2 stitches into the same hole so the plastic doesn't show. When you have gone all the way around the coaster, finish by leaving the thread on the back of the canvas after the last stitch, and weaving it behind the other stitches in the main part of the canvas for about $1/2$", working from the edge toward the center. Thread the beginning tail on the needle

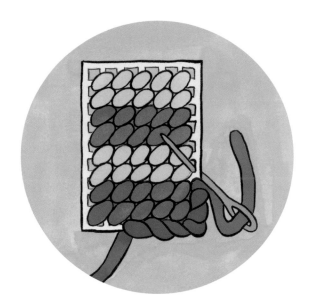

Step 4 **Whipstitch Coaster Edges**

and weave it under the stitches on the back of the work, too. Trim the ends of both tails to about $1/4$" long.

5 attach felt backing *(optional)*

Place the coaster on a piece of felt and trace all the way around the coaster. Using your fabric scissors, cut out the backing piece just inside the line, so the backing is a little bit smaller than the coaster, and will not show around the edges on the front. Following the directions on the fabric glue package, carefully glue the backing to the back of the coaster.

Coaster Charts

A needlepoint chart is like a map. Each small square represents a stitch. These charts show one of the color schemes for each coaster type shown on page 29: stripes, blocks, and flowers. Substitute your own choice of colors.

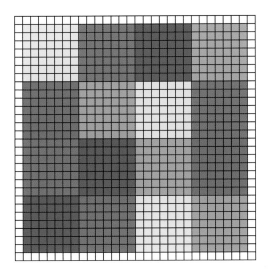

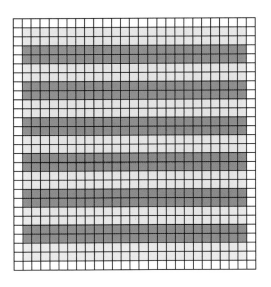

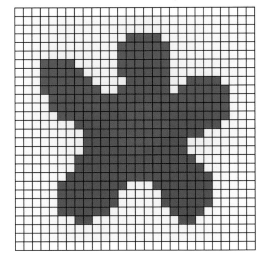

needlepoint
greeting **cards**

THESE CARDS are really two gifts in one. First, the needlepoint hearts and stars decorate the cards and make them special. Second, the needlepoint, with or without the paper card, can be framed. Or, the needlepoint can be glued like a patch onto a backpack or notebook, or turned into a refrigerator magnet by attaching magnetic tape (sold at craft stores) to the back.

    If you don't want to work from a chart, you can draw a simple shape of your own on the canvas with a permanent marker— star, flower, peace sign, or whatever you like—and stitch your shape as if you were coloring in a coloring book.

(1) prepare the canvas

For each card, cut a 4" square piece of plastic canvas, following the instructions on page 30. This is a bigger area than you will need for stitching; you will trim the extra canvas close to your stitching when you are finished.

Materials

1 ($10^1/_2$" X $13^1/_2$") PIECE PLASTIC CANVAS IN
   7 MESH SIZE (*this is enough to make 2 cards*)
2 (8-YARD) SKEINS PERSIAN WOOL,
   FOR BACKGROUND AND EDGING
1 (8-YARD) SKEIN PERSIAN WOOL IN A
   CONTRASTING COLOR, FOR CENTER DESIGN
SIZE 16 TAPESTRY NEEDLE
SCISSORS, FOR CUTTING PLASTIC CANVAS
2 ($8^1/_2$" X 11") PIECES CARD STOCK: ONE
   SHEET FOR BACKGROUND AND ONE SHEET
   IN A CONTRASTING COLOR FOR STRIPE
   (*For a special effect, choose a lighter weight
   handmade paper for the stripe.*)
ENVELOPE ($8^1/_2$" X $5^1/_2$"), OR SIZE TO FIT CARD
CRAFT GLUE

tent stitch • whipstitch

prepare the thread

Choose a color and thread your needle with 4 two-ply strands of wool (see Step 2 of Coaster instructions on page 30).

3 **needlepoint the heart or star**

Working in tent stitch (see page 26), needlepoint the heart or star from the charts on page 39. Count to where you want to begin stitching.

For the heart, begin 11 holes from the left and 3 holes up from the bottom.

For the star, begin 4 holes from the left and 3 holes up from the bottom.

To begin stitching, thread your needle and bring the thread up to the front through the correct hole, and pull the thread through, leaving a tail about 6" long on the back of the work to weave in later. Hold this tail against the back of the canvas as you take the first 3 or 4 stitches so it doesn't pull right through. After you have made a few stitches it will be anchored securely. Work the stitches in the first row of the chart; *for the heart* this will only be one stitch. For the star, work the 2 stitches of the lower left point.

Now, turn your work and the chart upside down, and work the next row. *For*

the heart, you will work 3 stitches centered on the first stitch. *For the star*, you will work 2 stitches but they will be moved over by one space to the left to correspond with the chart. Continue in this manner, turning the canvas and chart upside down every row in order to keep working from left to right. *For the star*, complete one point, then work the center, then build the other 4 points around the center.

When you get to the end of a section, or when there is about 5" of thread left, bring the thread to the back of the canvas and pull through. Secure the end by weaving it under the stitches on the back of the work for about $^1/_2$" as shown on page 31. To finish the tail from where you began stitching, thread the tail on a needle and weave it under the stitches on the back of the work for about $^1/_2$", too. Trim the ends of both tails to $^1/_4$" long. Prepare and start a new 4-strand length of yarn when you need it and continue until the shape is finished.

4 **needlepoint the background**

Prepare a 4-strand length of yarn for the background color and fill in all around the shape, starting and ending the thread as for the other sections. The colored part of the star and heart charts is 21 stitches wide and 21 stitches high, not counting the blank squares for the edging. Since your canvas is bigger than this, you will end the first row of the background color when it has 21 stitches, then turn the work upside down to continue. There will be some leftover canvas beyond the background. Just leave this part empty; you will trim it away when you get ready to finish the coaster.

5 *whipstitch around the edge of the needlepoint*

Trim the canvas and work whipstitch around the edge of the needlepoint as explained in Step 4 on page 34.

6 *make the paper card*

Fold the cardstock for the background in half so that it measures 8 $1/2$" tall and 5 $1/2$" wide. Cut the contrast card stock so that it measures 5 $3/4$" tall by 11", then fold it in half so that it measures 5 $3/4$" tall and 5 $1/2$" wide.

Slip the folded piece of contrasting card stock over the large piece with the folds at the same side. The contrasting paper should sit about in the middle of the main card, so that it looks like a wide stripe (see photo on page 37). Carefully glue the two pieces of paper together. Glue the needlepoint on top of the contrasting stripe as shown.

Greeting Card Charts

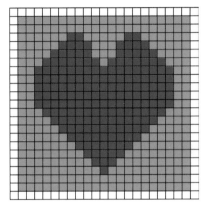

Heart

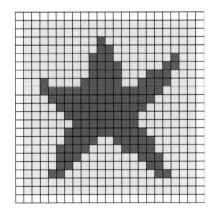

Star

Cross-Stitch

Cross-stitch is similar to needlepoint but
instead of making a single diagonal stitch,
you make two stitches that cross to form an X.
It is easy to learn cross-stitch on checked fabric like
gingham because the checks make a good guide as to
where to put the Xs. Later you can advance to what is
known as counted cross-stitch, which is worked on a
soft, solid-colored fabric called Aida cloth.

In colonial days, young girls were taught to
do cross-stitch at home or at school around the same
time they were taught to read and write.
They often learned the alphabet by working it
in cross-stitch, and they learned cross-stitch before
any of the other embroidery stitches.

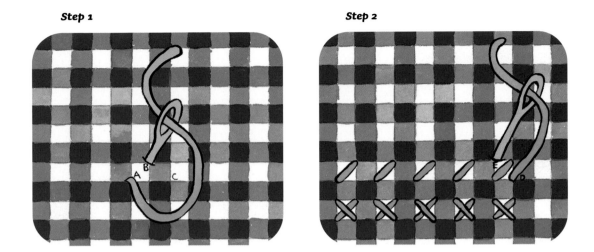

cross-stitch on gingham

FOR THE PROJECT IN THIS CHAPTER, YOU WILL MAKE CROSS-STITCHES
OVER THE WHITE SQUARES OF GINGHAM FABRIC.

STEP 1: Thread your needle and make a double knot in the end of the thread (see page 46). Bring the thread to the front of the fabric at A, in the lower left corner of a white check. Pull the thread through. Insert the needle at the upper right corner of the same white check at B, and pull the thread through to the back. Bring the needle back to the front of the fabric at C, at the bottom left corner of the next white square to the right, and pull the thread to the front. Continue stitching like this from left to right until the row is finished. The stitching will look like a line of diagonal stitches one square apart.

STEP 2: Bring the needle to the front in the lower right corner of the same white check where you stopped the previous row, marked D here. Insert the needle into the upper left corner of the same white check at E, and pull the thread to the back of the fabric to complete one cross. Continue working from right to left across the row to complete all the Xs.

To end the stitching, leave the thread on the back of the fabric after crossing the last stitch, and, right behind the last stitch, make a stitched knot (see page 46).

simple cross-stitch
pillow

GINGHAM FABRIC, sometimes simply called checked fabric, is very cheerful. Perhaps you've seen it used for kitchen curtains or as a tablecloth on a picnic table.

The design of these pillows is simple—a square of Xs is stitched inside the square shape of the pillow. Once you learn to cross-stitch on gingham, you can decorate store-bought gingham table runners, place mats, pillowcases, dresses, shirts— basically anything you can find made with this fun fabric. You may want to use an embroidery hoop when you are cross-stitching on gingham; the hoop makes it easier to embroider on the fabric and to keep the stitches even (to learn how to use a hoop, see page 48).

cross-stitch · running stitch · whipstitch

Materials

$1/2$-YARD 36" CHECKED GINGHAM FABRIC,
   WITH CHECKS THAT MEASURE $1/4$",
   $1/2$", OR $5/8$"
2 SKEINS EMBROIDERY FLOSS, IN A
   COLOR DARKER THAN THE DARKEST
   BOX IN YOUR FABRIC
WHITE SEWING THREAD FOR ASSEMBLING
   THE PILLOW
SIZE 1 SHARP-POINTED EMBROIDERY NEEDLE
SEWING NEEDLE
FABRIC SCISSORS
EMBROIDERY SCISSORS
POLYESTER FIBERFILL STUFFING,
   ENOUGH TO FILL YOUR PILLOW
RULER
WATER-SOLUBLE FABRIC MARKER IN A
   COLOR THAT WILL SHOW ON YOUR FABRIC
8" EMBROIDERY HOOP (*optional*)
PINS
THICK TOWEL, FOR BLOCKING

Did You Know?

The name gingham comes from a Dutch word, gingang, which is how the 17th-century Dutch traders pronounced a Malaysian word for striped cloth.

Starting and Stopping a Thread

TO MAKE SURE YOUR EMBROIDERY STITCHES DON'T COME UNDONE, IT'S IMPORTANT TO START AND END THE EMBROIDERY THREAD PROPERLY. FOR MANY OF THE PROJECTS IN THIS BOOK, YOU START WITH A DOUBLE KNOT AND END WITH A STITCHED KNOT.

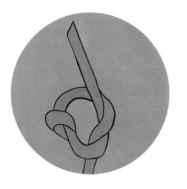

Starting with a Double Knot

To start with a double knot, after threading your needle, make two knots on top of each other at the end of your thread, then trim the tail to about ¼".
To begin embroidering, place the needle under the fabric and poke it through to the front side where you want to begin. Pull the threaded needle through until the knot catches on the back of the fabric.

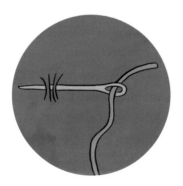

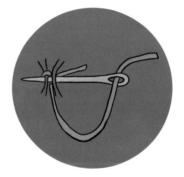

Stopping with a Stitched Knot

When you are finished with a piece of thread, turn the work over to the wrong side, and, right behind the last stitch so they won't show on the front, make 3 tiny, tight stitches on top of each other, making each stitch at a right angle to the one before. Trim the end of the thread to about ¼" long.

WRONG
SIDE

*Step 5 Pin and Sew Together Pillow
Front and Back; Trim Corners*

(5) sew the pillow front and back

Wash your finished embroidery according to
the instructions on page 49 to remove any
traces of the water-soluble marker and any
dirt that it may have picked up while you
were working.

Lay your embroidered piece flat on a
table with the right side of the embroidery
(the side without the knots) facing you. Place
the fabric square without any embroidery on
top. Using straight pins, pin the two pieces
together around all four sides. Thread a
36" length of white sewing thread and make
a double knot. With the sewing thread, sew

the two pieces together using a small
running stitch (see page 55) about $^{1}/_{8}$" long
and about $^{1}/_{2}$" in from the cut edge, leaving
a 5" opening in the middle of one side for
stuffing. If you follow the edge of the closest
line of gingham checks, your seams will be
perfectly even. If your thread runs short,
end it by making a stitched knot on the
seam line (just as you did to end the
cross-stitching), join a new strand of sewing
thread, and resume stitching the seam.
When you have finished sewing the seam,
trim the point off each corner. Removing this
excess fabric helps to make the pillow points
neat and sharp.

Using an Embroidery Hoop

To place fabric in an embroidery hoop, undo the screw that holds the two pieces of the hoop together. Put the smaller half of the hoop (without the screw) on a table. Lay the fabric on top of the circle with the area you will stitch in the center of the hoop. Push the larger half of the hoop (with the screw) down over the lower hoop and fabric. Tighten the screw a little bit so the fabric does not slide easily between the two hoops. Pull the fabric all the way around to make the center of the circle smooth and stretched tight, then fasten the screw the rest of the way so the fabric doesn't slip between the hoop at all anymore. When you finish embroidering the section in the hoop, remove the hoop by loosening the screw, and move the hoop to the next section you need to stitch.

When you finish stitching for the day, always remove your fabric from the hoop. If you don't, the hoop may create a permanent round wrinkle in the fabric.

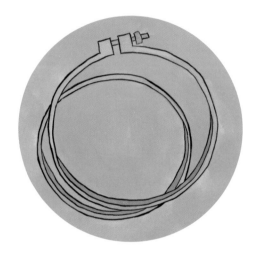

6 stuff and finish pillow

Turn the pillow right side out through the hole so that the embroidered side is facing you. To poke out the corners, use a blunt, pointed object like a knitting needle or the eraser end of a pencil, being careful not to poke through the fabric. With adult supervision, press the pillow with an iron, to neaten it. Stuff the pillow with fiberfill. To close the pillow opening, fold the raw fabric to the inside of the pillow using the check line you followed to seam your pillow pieces together as your guide. Pin the opening shut. Using whipstitch (see page 61), sew the opening of the pillow closed with stitches about $1/4$" long.

Step 6 Whipstitch the Pillow Closed

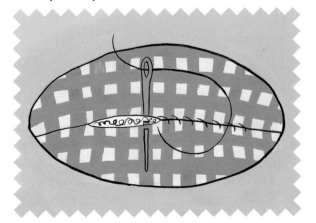

Finishing Your Embroidery

The last part of stitching most designs is finishing; this step is called blocking. When you block, you wet the fabric and pull it straight again. This removes any marks or wrinkles, and settles the stitches into their final position so they look even.

Fill a small, clean spray bottle with water. Place a thick bath towel on a flat surface like a table, stuffed chair, or mattress in an area where you can let your embroidery dry undisturbed. Lay the embroidery on the towel face up, and spray it with water so that it is damp all over. With your hands, gently pull the fabric straight, smooth, and flat. If necessary, place straight pins along the edges of the fabric to hold it in place until it is dry.

Embroidery Around the World

ALMOST EVERY CULTURE IN THE WORLD USES EMBROIDERY TO DECORATE CLOTHING AND HOUSEHOLD ITEMS. HERE ARE JUST A FEW EXAMPLES.

In Japan, kimonos and *obis* (sashes) are often decorated with a combination of embroidery and fabric painting.

The Chinese discovered the secret of making silk thread and fabric from silkworm cocoons and have used silk for embroidery for thousands of years. Satin stitches and knotted stitches are used frequently in traditional Chinese embroidery.

India and Pakistan have an amazing number of techniques and traditions for embroidery. *Shisha* embroidery is the most famous: small round mirror pieces are enclosed within embroidery stitches to make colorful, sparkly fabrics.

Because Afghanistan is one of the countries along the historic Silk Road, its embroidery includes materials and designs from many countries: silk from China, cotton from Pakistan and India, carpet motifs from other Middle Eastern countries. Nomadic tribes still decorate their clothing and animal gear with embroidery today.

Traditional embroidery throughout Eastern Europe features cross-stitch worked in red and black threads on white fabric, although different color schemes are used to indicate different regions.

Elaborate satin stitch floral embroidery is one of the first things people notice when they see traditional folk costumes from Scandinavia. These costumes were reinvented in the late 19th century by people wanting to explore and celebrate their national heritages. In Norway, embroidery shares many of the same floral motifs with a popular folk painting technique called *rosemaling*.

A traditional Native American type of embroidery called quillwork uses dyed, flattened porcupine quills stitched onto a tanned animal skin. Instead of thread, they use sinew (the tendons from the leg of deer, elk, or buffalo), which has to be chewed in order to stay soft enough for stitching.

Many people in Mexico and Guatemala still wear bright embroidered clothing everyday. The Guatemalan woman's blouse known as a *huipil* features motifs that may have historical meanings, such as flowers to represent the beauty and bounty of the earth.

India

Afghanistan

Native America

China

Japan

Mexico

Eastern Europe

Scandinavia

Basic
Freeform
Embroidery

Up to this point, you've been embroidering
single stitches for needlepoint and Xs for
cross-stitch on a grid, either on needlepoint mesh or
checked gingham fabric. With basic freeform stitches
you have a lot more choices. In fact, you can
embroider on just about any fabric in any direction.
Doing freeform embroidery is like drawing with yarn.
Think of the fabric as your paper and the
thread as your crayon.

The projects in this chapter use seven basic freeform
embroidery stitches. All of these stitches are called
straight stitches because by themselves they look
like straight lines of different lengths.

Practicing Freeform Embroidery

TO LEARN THE BASIC FREEFORM EMBROIDERY STITCHES, EITHER DIVE RIGHT INTO THE PROJECTS IN THIS CHAPTER AND LEARN AS YOU GO, OR PRACTICE EACH STITCH FIRST ON A PIECE OF PLAIN, SOLID-COLOR COTTON SCRAP FABRIC USING A 6-STRAND LENGTH OF EMBROIDERY FLOSS ABOUT 30" LONG, AND A LARGE-EYED, SHARP-POINTED EMBROIDERY NEEDLE.

Two Kinds of Stitches

MOST EMBROIDERY STITCHES CAN BE FORMED IN TWO STEPS OR IN A ONE-STEP SCOOPING MOTION. OFTEN IT IS EASIER TO LEARN A STITCH AS A TWO-STEP PROCESS; THEN, ONCE YOU GET THE HANG OF IT, YOU CAN EASILY SWITCH TO THE FASTER SCOOP STYLE.

Two-Step Stitch

Secure the thread with a double knot (see page 46). For the first step, bring the needle to the front side of the fabric and pull the thread through. For the second step, insert the needle, send it back to the underside of the fabric, and pull the thread through.

Scoop Stitch

Secure the thread with a double knot (see page 46). All in one motion, insert the needle in the fabric from front to back, and bring it back out on the front again, (like scooping a shovel full of sand from the beach), then pull up the thread.

Two-Step Running Stitch

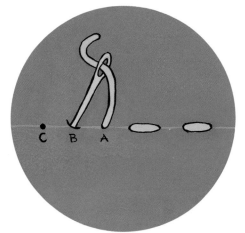

Scoop-Stitch Running Stitch

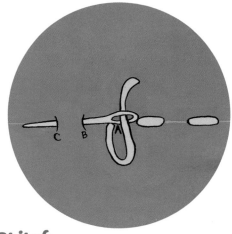

Running Stitch

RUNNING STITCH LOOKS LIKE THE DOTTED PASSING LINE IN THE MIDDLE OF THE ROAD. IT IS GOOD FOR OUTLINING SHAPES AND FOR MAKING DECORATIVE BORDERS. IT CAN ALSO BE USED TO SEW TOGETHER PIECES OF FABRIC.

To work as a two-step stitch, draw a straight or curvy line on a scrap of fabric. Your line of stitches will be following this line. Secure your thread on the back side of the fabric with a double knot (see page 46) and come up at A. Pull the thread through. Insert your needle at B, and pull your thread all the way through to the back of the work. Bring your needle up again at C, and pull the thread all the way through to the front side. Repeat until you have stitched the entire practice line.

To work as a scoop stitch, after you have pushed the needle down at B, scoop the fabric with the tip of your needle and come up at C in one motion. Pull the needle until the thread tightens. If the fabric puckers, you are pulling too tightly. Slip the point of your needle under the thread and loosen the stitch you just made so it lies flat, without pulling. Continue to stitch, following your practice line. Eventually, you will be able to take several stitches at a time before pulling the thread through.

For both methods, finish by taking the thread to the back side and weaving it under the stitches as shown on page 70. Trim the end, leaving a $1/4$" tail.

Seed Stitch

SEED STITCH IS A GROUP OF TINY STITCHES RANDOMLY PLACED CLOSE TOGETHER TO CREATE AN INTERESTING TEXTURE. IT CAN BE USED TO FILL SHAPES OR TO CREATE A SPOTTED SURFACE.

Secure your thread on the back side of the fabric with a double knot (see page 46) and come up at A. Pull the thread through. For a two-step stitch, insert your needle at B, and pull your thread all the way through to the back of the work. Bring your needle up again at C, and pull the thread all the way through to the front side.

Once you've practiced a little, you can work seed stitch in one step as shown here. After you have pushed the needle down at B, scoop the fabric with the tip of your needle and come up at C in one motion. Pull the needle until the thread tightens. Continue making the stitches at random, changing the direction of the stitches to look like scattered seeds. Finish by taking the thread to the back side and weaving it under the stitches as shown on page 70.

Backstitch

BACKSTITCH IS WORKED BEST AS A SCOOP STITCH. IT IS LIKE A DANCE WHERE YOU GO ONE STEP BACK, THEN TWO STEPS FORWARD. BACKSTITCH MAKES A NICE OUTLINE FOR CURVY SHAPES. IT CAN ALSO BE USED TO SEW TOGETHER TWO PIECES OF FABRIC BECAUSE IT IS VERY STRONG.

To practice, draw a circle on a scrap of cloth. Secure your thread on the back side of the fabric with a double knot (see page 46) and come up at A as shown in Figure 1 below. Pull the thread through. Move your needle backward to B and insert it, then bring it through to the front of the fabric at C with a single scooping motion. Pull the thread through. Insert the needle again at A and bring it to the front at D. Continue around the circle as shown in Figure 2. On the last stitch that closes the circle, finish by taking the thread to the back side and weaving it under the stitches as shown on page 70.

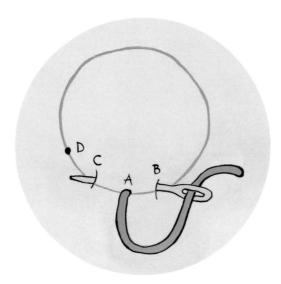

Figure 1

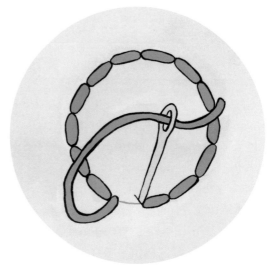

Figure 2

Figure 1 **Figure 2**

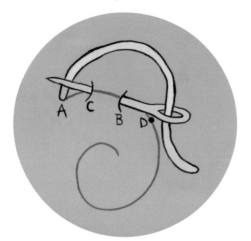
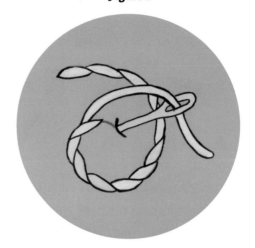

Stem Stitch

STEM STITCH IS ALSO SOMETIMES CALLED OUTLINE STITCH, AND IS WORKED AS A SCOOP STITCH. IT IS GOOD FOR STRAIGHT AND CURVY LINES, AND LOOKS A LITTLE THICKER THAN BACKSTITCH. IT IS FUN TO STITCH YOUR NAME IN STEM STITCH AS SHOWN ON THE AUTOGRAPH PILLOW ON PAGE 82.

Secure your thread on the back side of the fabric with a double knot (see page 46) and come up at A as shown in Figure 1. Pull the thread through. Working from right to left in a scooping motion, insert your needle into the fabric at B and come up at C (halfway between A and B), holding the thread down with your finger or thumb so it lies to one side of the needle. Pull the thread through. Keep the thread on the same side of the needle again, insert the needle at D, and bring the needle to the

front in the same hole at B. Pull through and continue.

Always hold the thread to the same side of the needle as you work, either on the top or the bottom. If you don't, your outline will look jagged instead of smooth. Try to make all the stitches the same size. Figure 2 shows how the curvy practice line will look when it's almost completed. Finish by taking the thread to the back side and weaving it under the stitches as shown on page 70.

Satin Stitch

SATIN STITCH IS SOMETIMES CALLED FILLING STITCH BECAUSE IT IS USED TO FILL IN LARGE SPACES AND TO MAKE SOLID SHAPES. THE STITCHES ARE WORKED VERY CLOSELY TOGETHER. YOU CAN WORK SATIN STITCHES ALL THE SAME LENGTH TO FILL STRAIGHT-EDGED SHAPES LIKE SQUARES, OR USE DIFFERENT-LENGTH STITCHES— STRAIGHT OR ON A SLANT—TO FILL CIRCLE, LEAF, OR FLOWER SHAPES. IT'S EASIEST TO LEARN SATIN STITCH AS A TWO-STEP STITCH, BUT AFTER YOU'VE GOTTEN THE HANG OF IT, YOU'LL PROBABLY WANT TO DO IT AS A SCOOP STITCH.

Secure your thread on the back side of the fabric with a double knot (see page 46) and come up at A. Pull the thread through. To work satin stitch in two steps, insert the needle to the back of the fabric at B and pull the thread through. Come to the front at C (right next to A), pull the thread through, and then insert the needle at D (right next to B) and pull the thread through.

To work satin stitch as a scoop stitch, insert the needle to the back of the fabric at A and bring to the front at B in one scooping motion.

If a stitch is too tight, slip the point of the needle under it and loosen so it lies flat.

For both methods, finish by taking the thread to the back side and weaving it under the stitches as shown on page 75.

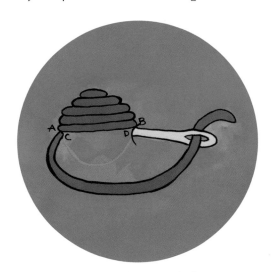

Two-Step Satin Stitch

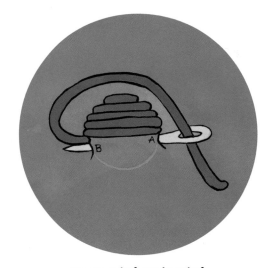

Scoop-Stitch Satin Stitch

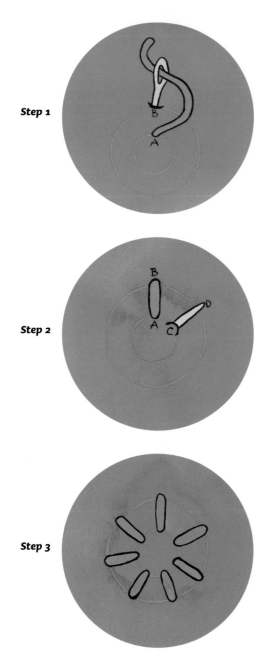

Step 1

Step 2

Step 3

Straight Stitch

STRAIGHT STITCH CAN BE USED TO FORM FLOWERS, TREES, SUN RAYS, OR ANY OTHER SHAPE YOU WANT. THIS EXAMPLE SHOWS A 7-POINTED SUNBURST THAT IS OPEN IN THE MIDDLE. IF YOU START BY DRAWING A SMALLER INSIDE CIRCLE, THEN YOU CAN MAKE THE POINTS ALMOST TOUCH AT THE CENTER.

STEP 1: To make a sunburst, draw two circles on your fabric, one inside the other. Secure your thread on the back side of the fabric with a double knot (see page 46) and come up at A. Pull the thread through. Insert the needle at B and pull the thread through to the back.

STEP 2: Bring the needle back to the front at C, and insert it again at D.

STEP 3: Continue around the circles until you have filled in the entire sunburst.

If your stitching is too tight, slip the point of your needle under the thread and loosen the stitch you just made so it lies flat, without pulling.

Finish by taking the thread to the back side and weaving it under the stitches as shown on page 70.

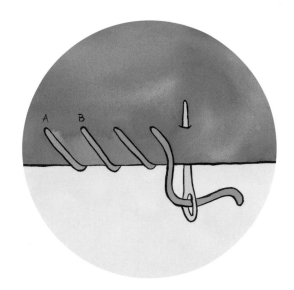

Whipstitch

WHIPSTITCH IS USED TO ENCLOSE THE EDGE OF A PROJECT WITH A SLANTED STITCH. IT IS VERY DECORATIVE, BUT IF THE STITCHES ARE WORKED CLOSE TOGETHER IT CAN ALSO BE USED TO SEW THE OPENING OF A PILLOW OR STUFFED TOY CLOSED. WHIPSTITCH TAKES PRACTICE, AND CAN BE MADE EASIER IF YOU MARK ALL YOUR STITCHING HOLES FIRST, USING A RULER OR TAPE MEASURE TO KEEP THEM EVEN. PLACE A SMALL DOT USING A WATER-SOLUBLE FABRIC MARKER AT EACH STITCH POINT. MAKE SURE THEY ARE ALL THE SAME DISTANCE FROM THE EDGE OF THE FABRIC, AND ALL THE SAME DISTANCE APART FROM EACH OTHER.

Secure your thread on the back side of the fabric with a double knot (see page 46) and come up at A. Pull the thread through. Hold the fabric with the edge you are enclosing nearest to you. Pull the needle toward you, tuck it under the fabric, and then poke it up through the fabric from back to front at B. Pull the thread through to the front side of the fabric. A diagonal line will form. Repeat however many times you like. The thread should lay flat. If your stitching is too tight, slip the point of your needle under the thread and loosen so the stitch you just made lies flat. Finish by taking the thread to the back side and weaving it under the stitches as shown on page 70.

felt needle case
with tie closure

EVEN THE MOST experienced embroiderers sometimes lose their needles if they don't have a special place to store them. This pretty needle case can quickly become your special place. It is made like a book with a cover, front and back flaps that act as pockets, four cloth pages, and a braided tie closure. You can use a different page for each size or type of needle to keep them separate, and the pockets on the cover can hold pins, thread, or a small needle threader.

(1) **cut the felt**

Cut three pieces of felt for the outside cover and pockets, as shown on page 64, according to the following measurements: for the outside cover, cut one piece of felt 3 1/2" x 5 1/2"; for the pockets on the inside flaps, cut 2 pieces 2 1/2" x 3 1/2". Using the other color of felt, for cloth pages, cut 2 pieces 5" x 3".

Materials

2 (9" X 12") PIECES OF FELT IN
    2 DIFFERENT COLORS
1 (8-YARD) SKEIN PERSIAN WOOL,
    OR 2 SKEINS EMBROIDERY FLOSS
    (shown in wool)
SIZE 22 CHENILLE NEEDLE
FABRIC SCISSORS
EMBROIDERY SCISSORS
RULER OR TAPE MEASURE
WATER-SOLUBLE FABRIC MARKER IN A COLOR
    THAT WILL SHOW ON YOUR FELT
PINS
THIN ($1/8$-INCH) PIECE OF RIBBON,
    TO BE USED INSTEAD OF THE
    BRAIDED-TIE CLOSURE *(optional)*
FABRIC GLUE, FOR ATTACHING TIE CLOSURE
    (optional)

running stitch

2) prepare the thread

Separate a single 2-ply strand of Persian wool about 32" long. If using embroidery floss, use all six strands for stitching, as it comes from the skein. See page 14 for instructions on preparing your thread.

3) attach the inside flap pockets

Referring to the top illustration on page 65, pin the inside flaps to each side of the cover, matching the edges and leaving a gap ¹/₂" wide in the center. You will stitch around the outside of the cover piece to join all the layers and create the inside pockets.

    Thread the needle with your prepared thread and make a double knot (see page 46) in the end. To hide the starting knot, insert the needle between the two layers of felt at a point about ¹/₈" in from one edge, then bring the needle up to the front.

    Work running stitches (see page 55) about ¹/₄" long and ¹/₄" apart, positioned about ¹/₈" in from the edge around all four sides. Finish by making a stitched knot (see page 46) in between the two layers of felt. Trim the end very close to the fabric so it won't stick out.

4) attach the pages

Pin the two inside pages exactly on top of each

Step 1 **Cut the Felt**

Cut 3 Pieces of Felt for Outside Cover and Pockets

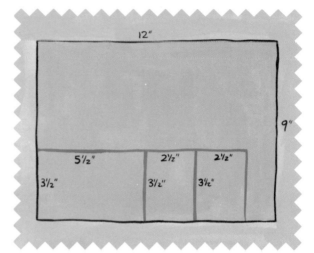

Cut Two Pieces of Felt for Cloth Pages

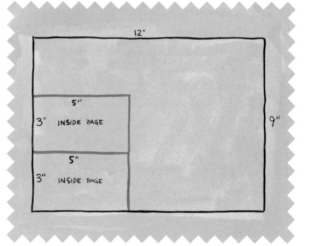

other. With the cover pocket-side up, place the pages on top of the cover, matching the center of the pages with the gap in the center of the cover as shown in the illustration below.

Thread the needle with your prepared thread and make a double knot in the end. To hide the starting knot, insert the needle between the two layers of felt at a point about $1/8$" in from one edge, between the outer page and the cover. Work running stitches $1/4$" long and $1/4$" apart, through all three layers straight down the center of the cover. Finish by bringing your thread to the inside between the cover and outer page. Make a stitched knot and trim the end very close to the fabric so it won't stick out. Fold the needle case closed like a book.

5 *make the tie closure*

Cut either a 3-strand length of Persian wool or a 6-strand length of embroidery floss 30" long. Knot all the pieces together very close to the end. Have a friend hold the knot and make a very tight 18-inch braid. Tie another knot to finish, then trim the ends very close to the knots. Fold the braid or optional ribbon tie in half and, using a dab of fabric glue, attach it to the center of the outside fold of the case. Or sew it to the case using several small stitches. Wrap half the tie around the front, half around the back, and tie shut.

Pin and Sew the Needle Case

Step 3 *Pin and Sew One Flap to Each Side of Cover*

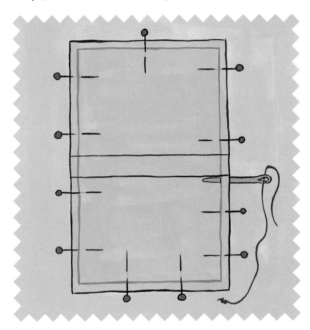

Step 4 *Pin and Sew the Pages to the Cover*

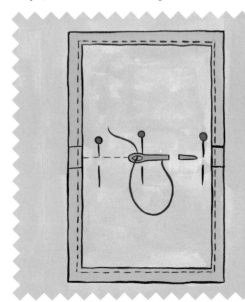

personal *pincushion*

A PINCUSHION IS LIKE A miniature pillow where you can safely store your pins. It can also be used to keep track of earrings and decorative pins to wear. Make a pincushion with the word "Pins" or star shapes stitched on it, as shown here, or stitch whatever you want—even your name (just like on the Autograph Pillows on page 82).

1 cut the felt

Cut 2 pieces of felt 5" x 7", as shown in the illustration on page 68. On one of the pieces of felt, with a water-soluble marker, draw a line ¹/₂" in from all four sides; this is the line you will sew on when you are attaching the front to the back of the pincushion.

2 prepare the yarn

Separate one 32-inch-long 2-ply strand of Persian wool from the other strands, following the instructions on page 14, and stitch using only one strand of wool thread. If using embroidery floss, prepare it according to the directions on page 14, and use all six strands for stitching, as it comes from the skein.

Materials
(for one pincushion)

1 (9" X 12") PIECE OF WOOL FELT
1 (8-YARD) SKEIN PERSIAN WOOL,
    OR 2 SKEINS EMBROIDERY FLOSS
    (shown in wool)
SIZE 22 CHENILLE NEEDLE
FABRIC SCISSORS
EMBROIDERY SCISSORS
RULER OR TAPE MEASURE
WATER-SOLUBLE MARKER OR DRESSMAKER'S
    TRACING PAPER IN A COLOR THAT WILL
    SHOW ON YOUR FELT
PINS
POLYESTER FIBERFILL STUFFING,
    SEVERAL HANDFULS

running stitch • straight stitch • backstitch

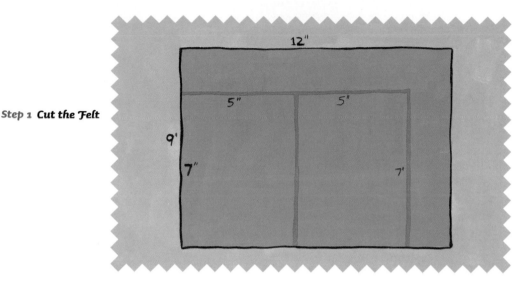

Step 1 Cut the Felt

③ embroider the pincushion

pins

Photocopy the "Pins" motif on page 141, enlarging it 245% so that the rectangle measures 5" x 7". Transfer the word "Pins" to the center of the piece of felt with the sewing outline drawn on it. Use either the window or tracing paper method (see page 71) to transfer the word to the felt.

Thread the needle with your prepared thread and make a double knot (see page 46) in the end. Begin stitching by coming up near the bottom curlicue at the base of the vertical line in the capital letter P. Use backstitch to stitch up to the top curlicue, and take the thread to the back of the fabric. Come up again near the top of the loop in the capital letter P, and backstitch to the end of the

curlicue that finishes the loop. End by taking the thread to the back side, and run the threaded needle through ¹/2" of stitches (see page 70). Trim the end to ¹/4". Start a new strand of thread at the top of the small letter I, and backstitch to the curlicue at the end of the letter S. End the thread as for the capital P. Start another strand and backstitch the swirl to dot the letter I. End the thread as for the rest of the word.

stars

With a water-soluble marker, draw six circles inside the sewing outline, about the size you want for each star. Inside each of these circles, draw a second, smaller circle, as for practicing a sunburst in the straight stitch instructions on page 60. Using straight stitch, stitch six stars with seven points each, as follows.

Thread the needle with your prepared thread and make a double knot (see page 46) in the end. Begin stitching by coming up to the front on the inner circle line. Take a straight stitch from the inner to the outer circle, and bring the thread to the back of the work to complete one point of the star. Come up again about $1/7$ of the way around the inner circle, and take another stitch to the outer circle like the first stitch. Work around the star until all seven points have been completed. End by taking the thread to the back side, and run the threaded needle

through $1/2$" of stitches (see page 70). Trim the end to $1/4$". Start a new strand of thread for each of the other stars, and end each star the same as the first.

(4) *finish the pin cushion*

Pin both pieces of felt together with the embroidered side facing you. Thread the needle with your prepared thread and make a double knot in the end. To hide the starting knot, insert the needle between the two layers of felt about 2" in from one of the long corners on the sewing line, as shown in the illustration below. Work

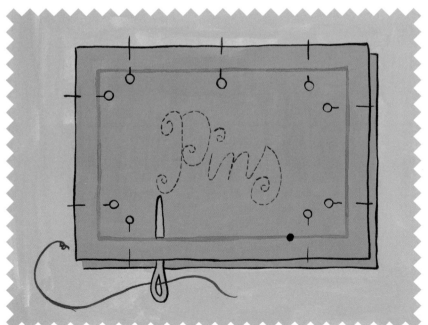

Step 4 *Pin and Sew the Felt*

running stitches, about $1/8$" long and $1/8$" apart, along the sewing line through both layers, removing the pins as you go. Try to make all of your stitches the same length. When you have worked around four sides, stop about 3" from where you began, but don't end the thread.

If you run short of thread while you are stitching, finish by taking the thread through the top layer only and end the thread by making a stitched knot (see page 46). Trim the end very close to the fabric so it won't stick out the side. Begin your next thread with its knot sandwiched in between the two layers like before.

When you get to about 3" from where you began stitching, park your threaded needle in the top layer of the pincushion to hold it. Carefully stuff the pincushion so that it is very full and firm, using the eraser end of a pencil to help poke the stuffing inside. When you are happy with how it feels, stitch to the end of the seam. Finish by taking the thread through the top layer only, and make a stitched knot, between the layers and on top of one of the running stitches, so it will not show. Trim the end very close to the fabric so it won't stick out the side. Spray lightly or dab the sewing line with water to remove all traces of the water-soluble marker.

Ending a Thread Through Back Side of Stitches

To end a thread in freeform embroidery, after your last stitch, take the thread to the back side of the fabric and turn your work over. Run the threaded needle through $1/2$" of stitches, then trim the end to $1/4$" long.

Transferring Designs to Fabric

BEFORE YOU BEGIN STITCHING, YOU MAY WANT TO TRANSFER A DESIGN TO YOUR FABRIC. FOR THE PROJECTS IN THIS BOOK, YOU CAN USE THE WINDOW TRACING METHOD OR THE TRACING PAPER METHOD.

for both methods

Make a photocopy of the design, increasing it in size if needed, or draw it on a piece of paper. Cut around the outside of the design, leaving a 1/4" border of blank paper all around. The border makes it easier to handle the design and place it where you want it on your fabric.

for window tracing

Tape the motif to a sunny window, then tape the fabric on top of it so the sun shines through both the paper and the fabric. Make sure the design is positioned where you want it on your fabric, moving the fabric around if necessary. With a water-soluble marker (if you need to remove the marks later) or with a pencil (if you will be covering the marks completely), trace the design onto the fabric using a color of marker or pencil that will show. You can also use a sharp-pointed piece of chalk for tracing and then carefully brush away all traces of the chalk when you have finished.

tracing paper method

This method uses dressmaker's tracing paper, which is available at fabric, quilting, and craft stores. Each package usually includes several different colors. Choose a color that will show up well on your embroidery fabric. For instance, if your fabric is dark blue, use white tracing paper.

Lay your fabric on a hard, flat surface and place the tracing paper on top of the fabric with the waxy side down, then place your paper design on top of the tracing paper. Make sure the design is positioned where you want it on your fabric. Pin all 3 layers (fabric, tracing paper, design paper) together so they don't shift. Using a ballpoint pen, trace right on top of the lines of the design, pressing firmly. When you are finished, the design will be on the fabric.

old-fashioned
cats & dogs

THESE SOFT PETS LOOK a little old-fashioned, as though they might have belonged to boys and girls who lived a long time ago and played with handmade toys. If you want your animals to look more realistic, use fur colors like gray, black, or tan.

(1) *enlarge the pattern*

Decide whether you want to make a dog or a cat. Photocopy the pattern for the animal you want to make (see page 141), enlarging it 230%. The enlarged pattern will fit on an 8 1/2" x 11" piece of paper. If you like, you can draw your own dog or cat instead of using the ones shown here. Just be sure that your design will fit on the piece of felt.

Materials *(for one animal)*

2 (9" X 12") PIECES FELT

2 (8-YARD) SKEINS PERSIAN WOOL,
   ONE DARK COLOR FOR FACE AND OUTSIDE
   SEAM, AND A LIGHTER ACCENT COLOR
   FOR THE EYES

SIZE 22 CHENILLE NEEDLE

FABRIC SCISSORS

EMBROIDERY SCISSORS

CRAFT SCISSORS

RULER OR TAPE MEASURE

WATER-SOLUBLE MARKER OR PENCIL IN A
   COLOR THAT WILL SHOW ON YOUR FELT

DRESSMAKER'S TRACING PAPER IN A COLOR
   THAT WILL SHOW ON YOUR FELT *(optional)*

PINS

POLYESTER FIBERFILL STUFFING,
   SEVERAL HANDFULS

running stitch · backstitch · satin stitch

2. cut out the animal

Using craft scissors, cut around the enlarged dog or cat shape to make a pattern; if you are making the dog, don't forget to cut the separate piece for the ear. Place one of your pieces of felt on a flat surface safe for cutting. Pin the pattern to the fabric and cut around it using fabric scissors. Unpin the pattern and repeat for the other piece of felt to make the second side of the animal. For the dog, cut 2 ears.

3. transfer the eyes, nose, and mouth

Using the window or tracing paper method (see page 71), transfer the eyes, nose, and mouth from the paper pattern to one piece of fabric for the cat, and to both pieces of fabric for the dog. Trace the dog faces so the two dog pieces are facing different directions; when you sew them together they will make the two sides of the same dog.

4. embroider the eyes

Separate two 2-ply strands of the dark Persian wool about 32" long, following the instructions on page 14. Thread the needle with the two strands and make a double knot (see page 46) in the end of the thread. Begin stitching by coming up at one side of

the pupil of the eye, and fill in the pupil with satin stitch (see page 59). End by taking the thread to the back side, and run the threaded needle through the back of the satin stitches as shown at right. Trim the end to $1/4$". Start two strands of the accent color for the iris and anchor them as for the pupil. Use satin stitch to fill in the iris, making each stitch begin at the edge of the pupil and end at the edge of the outline around the outside of the eye. End the thread as for the pupil. Start two new strands of dark thread for the outside of the eye, and work backstitch (see page 57) all the way around the outer circle. End by taking the thread to the back side, running the threaded needle through $1/2$" of stitches (see page 70), and trimming the end to $1/4$". Make both eyes on the front piece of the cat, and make an eye on each piece for the dog.

5. embroider the nose and mouth

Thread the needle with two strands of the dark color and make a double knot in the end of the thread. Begin stitching by coming up at one side of the nose, and fill in the nose with satin stitch. End the thread as for the pupil and iris. Start a new thread and embroider the lines for the mouth and around the outer edge of nose in backstitch. End the thread as before. For the dog, work the nose and mouth on the other piece.

6   add the cat's whiskers

If you are making a cat, thread the needle with the dark color and make a small, single stitch (less than $1/8$" long) near one bottom corner of the cat's nose, leaving a tail about $2\,1/2$" long. Cut the end of the thread attached to the needle so it sticks out $2\,1/2$" on the other side of the stitch. Take the two ends and tie them tightly in a double knot to secure the whisker. Make more whiskers the same way on each side of the nose. Trim them until you are happy with how they look.

7   make the dog's ears

If you are making a dog, thread the needle with two strands of the dark color and make a double knot in the end of the thread. Begin stitching at the top of one ear piece, and work running stitches, about $1/8$" long, $1/8$" apart, and $1/8$" in from the edge, all the way around the curved edge of the ear and back up to the straight edge of the top. End the thread with a stitched knot. Do not stitch across the straight edge. Repeat for the other ear.

Ending a Thread for Satin Stitch

To end a thread for satin stitch, after your last stitch, take your thread to the back side of the fabric and turn your work over. Run the threaded needle under approximately six stitches, then double it back under the last stitch; to finish, run the needle under about six more stitches, then trim the end to $1/4$" long.

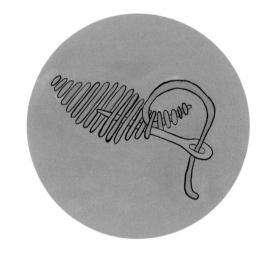

(8) *assemble animal*

Each animal is sewn together all around its outside edges with $1/8$" running stitches. The stitching both decorates the edge of the animal, and also holds the two halves together so they can be stuffed.

Pin both pieces of felt with the embroidered sides facing out. For the dog, pin one ear to the head on each side. Thread the needle with two strands of the dark color and make a double knot in the end of the thread. For the dog, begin stitching at the upper back, just before the tail. For the cat, begin stitching at the bottom of the cat on the inside of the left leg. To hide the starting knot, insert the needle between the two layers of felt about $1/8$" away from one edge. Work running stitches, about $1/8$" long, $1/8$" apart, and $1/8$" from the edge through all layers, removing the pins as you go. Try to make all of your stitches the same length. When you have worked almost all the way around, stop about 3" from where you began, but don't end the thread.

If you run short of thread while you are stitching, finish by taking the thread through the top layer only, and make a stitched knot (see page 46) on top of one of the running stitch threads, so it will not show on the outside. Trim the end very close to the fabric so it won't stick out the side. Begin your next thread with its knot sandwiched in between the two layers like before.

When you get to 3" from where you began, park your threaded needle in the top layer of the animal to hold it. Carefully stuff the animal as full as you want it, using the eraser end of a pencil to help poke the stuffing into the corners, then, stitch to the end of the seam. Finish by taking the thread through the top layer only, and make a stitched knot on top of one of the running stitch threads, so it will not show. Trim the end very close to the fabric so it won't stick out the side. Spray lightly or dab the sewing line with water to remove all traces of the water-soluble marker.

Imagine That!

While the gold cat and red dog were made with felt from the fabric store, the other cat and dog were made from recycled and felted fabric. The plaid cat started out as a coat; the gold dog used to be a sweater. For more on recycling, see page 22.

whipstitch
lampshade

FOR THIS PROJECT, a plain lampshade is
dressed up with whipstitch. You might already
have a lampshade in your room that you can
decorate with stitching. Pick a fun color and go!

 1 *prepare the yarn and lampshade*

Cut a piece of Persian yarn about 40" long.
Make a double knot (see page 46) about 4"
from one end.

    Work only with the lampshade, not
the entire lamp. With the tape measure and
water-soluble marker, place small dots $^1/_2$" up
from the bottom edge of the shade and $^3/_4$"
apart around the bottom of the lampshade
until you are about 4" away from where you
began. Look along the tape measure to see if
you will end right at the first dot by continuing
to make marks $^3/_4$" apart. If not, make your
last few marks a little closer or a little farther
apart so they look even and end at the first
dot. Make the dots very small so that they will
be easy to remove with just a tiny dab of water
when you are finished. Repeat for the upper
edge of the shade, placing dots $^1/_2$" down from
the top and $^3/_4$" apart all the way around, and
adjusting the last few dots if needed.

Materials

FABRIC OR PAPER LAMPSHADE, ONE LAYER THICK

2 (8-YARD) SKEINS PERSIAN WOOL,
   OR ABOUT 16 YARDS KNITTING YARN

SIZE 18 CHENILLE NEEDLE

EMBROIDERY SCISSORS

TAPE MEASURE

WATER-SOLUBLE MARKER IN A COLOR THAT
   WILL SHOW ON YOUR LAMPSHADE

whipstitch

Lots of Choices!

Embroidery can be done on any surface—baskets, purses, backpacks, note-books—even lampshades. The only requirement is that you can poke a threaded needle through the item, so while a wooden box won't work, a cardboard box will!

3 *embroider the lampshade*

Start stitching near the seam of the shade at the bottom edge. Poke needle from the inside to the outside at one of the dots until the knot catches on the back side. To make next stitch, bring needle to the inside of the shade and poke it through from inside to outside again at the next mark. Work whipstitches around the shade as shown on page 61. Do not pull the stitches too tightly, but keep them snug and neat. Continue until about 5" or 6" of yarn remains, and finish by taking the thread to the inside of the shade. Unthread the needle, and leave the old end hanging loose. Thread a new 40" strand, and tie the end of the new yarn to the loose end of the old yarn as close as possible to the inside surface of the shade. Leave the tails hanging loose for now. Continue stitching until the entire edge is covered with whipstitches. When you arrive back where you began, poke the thread to the inside of the shade, and tie the end of the working thread to the beginning tail as close as possible to surface of the shade. Trim all the ends to ¹/₄" long. Repeat for the top edge of the shade. Carefully dab any dots that show with a tiny amount of water on your fingertip to remove all traces of the water-soluble marker. Place the lampshade on your lamp.

Embroidering Your Own Artwork

Make your own very special artwork by transforming one of your own paintings to fabric and embroidering over it.

Scan the painting into your computer and print it out on fabric transfer paper (sold at craft and office supply stores). If you don't have a computer, ask a copy shop to photocopy your design onto transfer paper.

Handle the printed transfer paper carefully so the color doesn't crack or flake off. Follow the directions on the transfer paper package to iron the design onto smooth, tightly woven cotton muslin. When the design is completely transferred, peel off the paper backing, and allow the fabric to cool. Decorate your artwork with your favorite stitches, then frame.

Embroidery Explorations

Embroidery has been practiced for thousands of years. To see samples made long
ago and far away, visit history, art, textile, and folk museums. Your local historical
society may even have samples of embroidery that were made in your town.
If no one in your family knows how to embroider and you need help, ask a teacher
or librarian if they know someone who can assist you. Also try your local needlework, craft,
or fabric stores for classes. To find the nearest stores, look in the Yellow Pages.
Start your own embroidery club so you and your friends can share your skills and ideas.
Long ago these kinds of clubs were called sewing circles or quilting bees and
were very popular; each neighborhood had one or more groups.

Visit some of the many sites on the Internet that feature information about embroidery.
Here are some fun sites to get you started:

www.planetc.com/users/derwyddon/emblinks.htm

www.dmc-usa.com

www.cross-stitching.com

www.doverpublications.com

www.freeembroiderystuff.com

www.historic-deerfield.org

www.white-works.com/histembam.htm

www.needleworksamplers.com

www.museumfortextiles.on.ca

To learn more embroidery techniques, check out the books
at your local library or bookstore. There are thousands of stitches you can
learn after you master the basics.

autograph **pillow**

DECORATE YOUR ROOM with these cool
pillows or give them as gifts. You can stitch
whatever designs you want on a pillow,
like your name as shown here, or even a
saying, a poem, or a monogram. For more
about monograms, see page 85.

 1 *cut the felt*

Cut two pieces of felt, each 14" square.
On one of the pieces of felt, with a water-
soluble marker, draw a line 1" in from all
four sides; this will be your sewing line
when you sew the front and the back of
the pillow together.

2 *prepare the yarn*

Separate a single 2-ply strand of Persian wool
about 32" long, following the instructions
on page 14. You will stitch using only one
strand of thread.

Materials *(for one pillow)*

$^1/_2$-YARD 45" OR 54" WIDE FELT

1 (8-YARD) SKEIN PERSIAN WOOL

SIZE 22 CHENILLE NEEDLE

FABRIC SCISSORS

EMBROIDERY SCISSORS

RULER OR TAPE MEASURE

WATER-SOLUBLE MARKER OR DRESSMAKER'S
TRACING PAPER IN A COLOR THAT WILL
SHOW ON YOUR FELT

PINS

POLYESTER FIBERFILL STUFFING, ENOUGH TO
STUFF A PILLOW FIRMLY

stem stitch • running stitch

Easy Do-Overs!

Write your name in water-soluble marker before you embroider it. That way you can easily erase it and try again if you don't like how it looks.

3 prepare the design

In the center of one piece of felt, using a water-soluble marker, write your name in large letters. If you don't like how your name looks, spray lightly or dab the line with water to remove it. Wait for the felt to dry before writing your name again because the water-soluble marker will not work on wet fabric. You can use a hair dryer to speed up the process.

4 embroider your name

Thread the needle with a single 2-ply strand of Persian wool and make a double knot (see page 46) in the end. Begin stitching by coming up at the end of one letter, and use stem stitch (see page 58) to complete as much of the name as you can in one continuous line of stitching. End by taking the thread to the back side, and run the threaded needle through $^{1}/_{2}$" of stitches (see page 70). Trim the end to $^{1}/_{4}$". Start a new strand of thread as needed, and continue until the entire name has been completed. When stitching around curves, work the stitches very small and close together for a neat, tight curve.

The Autograph Pillow is a great project for a group of friends to work on together.

5 assemble the pillow

Pin both pieces of felt together with the embroidered side facing you. Thread the needle with a single 2-ply strand of Persian wool and make a double knot in the end. To hide the starting knot, insert the needle between the two layers of felt about 3" away from one of the corners, and come up to the front on the sewing line. Work running stitches (see page 55), about $^{1}/_{4}$"

long and $1/4$" apart, along the sewing line through both layers, removing the pins as you go. Try to make all of your stitches the same length. Stop when you have worked all the way around all four sides except for the last 4", but don't end the thread.

If you run short of thread while you are stitching, finish by taking the thread through the top layer only and making a stitched knot (see page 46) between the two layers so it will not show. Trim the end very close to the fabric so it won't stick out the side. Begin your next thread with its knot sandwiched in between the two layers.

When you get to 4" from the end of the last side, park your threaded needle in the top layer of the pillow to hold it. Carefully stuff the pillow as full as you want it. When you are happy with how it feels, stitch to the end of the seam. Finish by taking the thread through the top layer only and making a stitched knot between the two layers so it will not show. Trim the end very close to the fabric so it won't stick out the side. Spray lightly or dab the sewing line with water to remove all traces of the water-soluble marker.

Making a Monogram

Instead of autographing your pillow with your whole name, you might want to use a really big initial, like a big J if your name is Julia or a big B if your name is Ben. Monogram is a fancy word for a really big initial

You can write your monogram by hand, or for more variety you can use a computer. Type your initial into the computer, enlarge it as much as you like, and try out different fonts (lettering styles) to find the one you think looks the best. Print out your initial and, using one of the transfer methods shown on page 71, transfer it to your pillow or whatever project you like. If your monogram is very thick, you might want to consider working it in satin stitch, instead of stem stitch. Monograms look great on pillowcases, towels, backpacks, handkerchiefs, and other personal items.

felt journal cover

MAKE ANY NOTEBOOK look special by adding its very own embroidered cover. Choose one of the motifs on page 141 or make up one of your own.

1) cut the felt

Open the notebook and place it at the lower right-hand corner of the felt you will use for the cover, about $1/4$" in from both edges (see Figure A on page 88). Place a mark on the felt $1/4$" above the top of the notebook. Using a ruler and water-soluble marker, draw a straight line across the felt at the mark. Cut the felt along this line for the top edge of the journal cover.

Place the notebook on top of the cut piece of felt again (see Figure B). With two small pieces of tape, gently tape the felt to the notebook along the right-hand side, leaving $1/4$" border of felt along the top, bottom, and right edge. Close the notebook, folding the piece of cover felt around it (see Figure C). With the notebook still closed, mark $1/4$" past where the back cover of the notebook ends on the felt.

Materials

SMALL NOTEBOOK (*approximately 4" x 5 $1/2$"*)

TWO (9" X 12") PIECES OF FELT, IN 2 DIFFERENT COLORS

1 (8-YARD) SKEIN PERSIAN WOOL, IN A COLOR DARKER THAN YOUR FELT

SIZE 22 CHENILLE NEEDLE

FABRIC SCISSORS

EMBROIDERY SCISSORS

RULER OR TAPE MEASURE

WATER-SOLUBLE FABRIC MARKER IN A COLOR THAT WILL SHOW ON YOUR FELT

PENCIL OR BALLPOINT PEN

DRESSMAKER'S TRACING PAPER IN A COLOR THAT WILL SHOW ON YOUR FELT (*optional*)

PINS

TAPE

---

running stitch • backstitch
seed stitch • satin stitch

Remove the notebook and tape, and draw a straight line at the mark to indicate the other side edge of the journal cover. Cut along this line. For the inside flaps, measure the height of the cover piece, and from the other piece of felt, cut two pieces the same height as the cover and 2 3/4" wide, as shown in Figure D.

(2) *transfer your design*

Choose one of the motifs on page 141 to embroider on the front of your notebook cover and make a photocopy of it, enlarging it by 175%. Or, draw your own design with a dark marker on a piece of paper. Position the design by folding the felt around the notebook, then pinning the motif where you want it. Using either the window or tracing paper method (see page 71), transfer the design to the felt. If the transfer markings aren't dark enough, use the water-soluble marker to draw on top of them.

Step 1 *Measure and Cut the Felt*

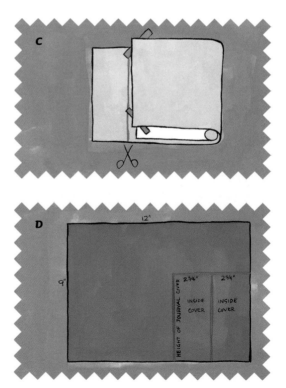

3 embroider the design

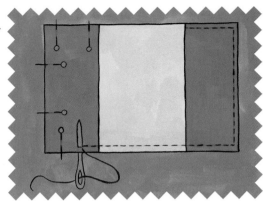

Separate a single 2-ply strand of Persian wool about 32" long, following the instructions on page 14. Thread the needle with the single strand and make a double knot (see page 46) in the end. Bring the thread to the front along one of the lines you drew for your design, and backstitch (see page 57) along the line using small stitches about $^1/8$" long. For the sprinkles on the ice cream and the roof of the house, use seed stitch (see page 56). Fill in the pedals, seat, and handles of the bike with satin stitch (see page 59). End by taking the thread to the back side and running it through $^1/2$" of stitches (see page 75). Trim the end to $^1/4$". Start and end new strands as needed until you have completed embroidering your design.

4 pin and sew the journal cover

Using the water-soluble marker and a ruler, draw a line $^1/4$" in from the edge around all four sides of the cover piece on the outside of the journal. Place an inside flap piece at each of the short ends of the cover as shown in the illustration above. Pin the flaps to the cover. You will stitch all the way around the outside of the cover piece to attach the inside flaps.

Thread the needle and make a double knot in the end. To hide the starting knot, insert the needle between the two layers of felt (cover and flap) about $^1/4$" in from one edge, then bring the needle up to the front. Work running stitches (see page 55) about $^1/4$" long and $^1/4$" apart along the line drawn around all four sides. Finish by taking the thread through the top layer only and making a stitched knot (see page 46) on top of one of the running stitches so it won't show. Trim the end so it won't stick out.

Dab or spray the sewing lines with water to remove the water-soluble marker. Place a thick towel on a flat surface like a table or mattress in an area where the journal cover won't be disturbed. Lay the cover on the towel face up, and spray it with water so that it is damp all over. With your hands, gently pull the fabric straight, smooth, and flat. If necessary, pin the journal to the towel along the edges to hold it in place. When dry, insert the notebook into the cover by slipping the back and front covers under the inside flaps.

Looped Stitches

Probably when you were first experimenting
with freeform stitching in the last chapter,
you found yourself accidentally catching a thread
when you weren't supposed to and forming a loop or a
knot. For the stitches in this chapter—called looped
stitches—you create a loop of thread on purpose.
Looped stitches are more decorative than straight
stitches. You can combine them with straight stitches
to make intricate embroideries or use them on their
own to make simpler projects.

Blanket Stitch

BLANKET STITCH LOOKS LIKE A BUNCH OF j's HOOKED TOGETHER. YOU CAN CHANGE THE LENGTHS OF THE j's OF BLANKET STITCH TO MAKE UP YOUR OWN PATTERNS—1 SHORT, 1 LONG, OR WHATEVER YOU CAN DREAM UP. BLANKET STITCH CAN BE WORKED ON THE MAIN AREA OF YOUR FABRIC, LIKE OTHER STITCHES, OR ALONG THE EDGE OF THE FABRIC TO DECORATE IT AND/OR BIND IT SO IT WILL NOT FRAY. IF YOU WORK BLANKET STITCHES VERY CLOSE TOGETHER, IT BECOMES BUTTONHOLE STITCH, THE STITCH USED TO MAKE BUTTONHOLES BEFORE SEWING MACHINES WERE INVENTED.

Working Blanket Stitch on Fabric

Secure your thread on the back side of the fabric using a double knot (see page 46) and come up at A. Pull the thread all the way through. Working from left to right, insert your needle down into the fabric at B and make a scooping stitch to bring it to the front at C. Make sure the thread is looped under the needle when you pull the needle through, and a J-shaped loop will form. Repeat the scoop stitch at the B and C positions to make the next stitch. Space the stitches evenly.

Figure 2 shows a straight line of blanket stitches made from left to right. Continue until you have worked all the blanket stitches you want. To finish, insert your needle down into the fabric at the corner of the last j, and weave it under the stitches on the back side as shown on page 70. Trim the end, leaving a ¹/₄" tail.

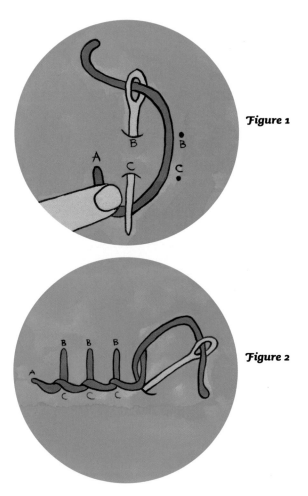

Figure 1

Figure 2

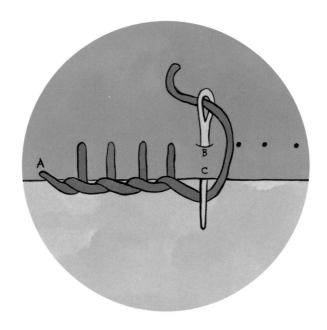

Working Blanket Stitch Along an Edge

When you are working blanket stitch along the edge of a project, as for the Blanket Stitch Scarf on page 98, secure your thread on the back side of the fabric with a double knot (see page 46) very close to the edge and come up at A. Pull the thread all the way through. Working from left to right, insert your needle down into the fabric at B and make a scooping stitch to bring it out just beyond the edge. Make sure the thread is looped under the needle when you pull the needle through, and a j-shaped loop will form. Carefully pull the thread all the way through until the j-shaped loop just touches the edge of the fabric. Space the stitches evenly.

If you pull too hard and the edge puckers, slip your needle under the thread and loosen it so the thread lays flat. Finish by taking the thread to the back side at the corner of the last j, as shown in Figure 2 at left, and weave it under the stitches on the back side as shown on page 70. Trim the end, leaving a $1/4$" tail.

Figure 1 **Figure 2**

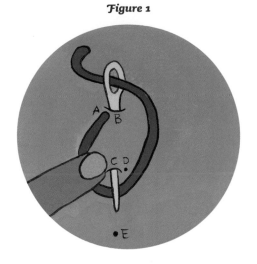

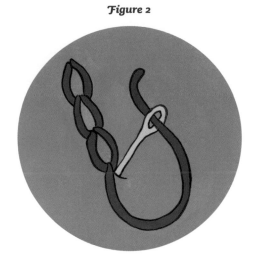

Chain Stitch

CHAIN STITCH IS A LOT OF FUN. IT GOES QUICKLY, AND CAN BE USED EITHER FOR OUTLINING OR FILLING IN SHAPES. IT LOOKS NICE IN CIRCULAR AND NATURAL-SHAPED MOTIFS SUCH AS FLOWERS, LEAVES, AND ANIMALS.

Secure your thread on the back side of the fabric with a double knot (see page 46) and come up at A. Pull the thread through. Insert your needle down into the fabric at B and make a scooping stitch to bring it to the front at C. Make sure the thread is looped around the needle when you pull the needle through. Carefully pull the thread all the way through to form a loop like a link in a chain. To make the next chain stitch, insert the needle into the fabric at D as close to C as possible without going into the same

hole, and take another scoop stitch from D to E, catching the thread loop under the needle as before.

Continue stitching until you have worked all the chain stitches you want. To finish, insert your needle down into the fabric just below the bottom edge of the last chain, taking a small stitch to anchor the bottom of the last loop, as shown in Figure 2. Finish by weaving the thread under the stitches on the back side as shown on page 70. Trim the end, leaving a $1/4$" tail.

Lazy Daisy

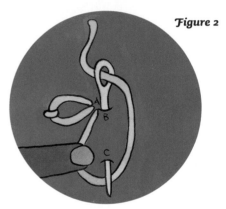

Figure 1

THE LAZY DAISY IS ACTUALLY A GROUP OF SEPARATE CHAIN STITCHES ARRANGED IN A CIRCLE TO LOOK LIKE A FLOWER, WITH THE INDIVIDUAL CHAIN STITCHES FORMING THE PETALS. IT IS SOMETIMES CALLED DETACHED CHAIN STITCH. YOU CAN ALSO WORK CHAIN STITCHES SEPARATELY ON EITHER SIDE OF A LINE OF STEM STITCHES, AND THEY WILL LOOK LIKE LEAVES ALONG A STEM.

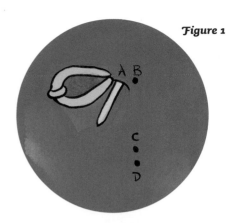

Figure 2

Figure 1 shows one lazy daisy stitch completed, and the points A, B, C, and D marked for making the second chain stitch. To make a stitch, secure your thread on the back side of the fabric using a double knot (see page 46), and come up where you would like to begin (for the first stitch), or come up at A next to the first stitch. Pull the thread through. As shown in Figure 2, insert your needle down into the fabric at B, and make a scooping stitch to bring it to the front at C. Make sure the thread is looped around the needle when you pull the needle through. Carefully pull the thread all the way through to form a loop like a link in a chain. To anchor the bottom of the loop, take a small stitch by inserting the needle at D as shown in Figure 3.

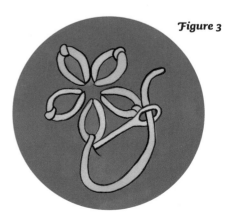

Figure 3

Work individual chain stitches around in a circle, anchoring the bottom of each loop with a small stitch, and always beginning each chain stitch close to the center of the flower. The petals of the flower will radiate around the center with the points A and B of each petal close together.

Feather Stitch

FEATHER STITCH IS SIMILAR TO CHAIN STITCH, BUT IT HAS A MORE OPEN LOOK TO IT. WORKING FEATHER STITCH IS LIKE DOING A SQUARE DANCE WHERE THE THREADS SWING FROM SIDE TO SIDE OF AN IMAGINARY LINE. WHEN WORKED WITH LOTS OF SPACE BETWEEN THE STITCHES, FEATHER STITCH HAS A DECORATIVE APPEARANCE LIKE A FERN PLANT OR CORAL IN THE OCEAN. IT CAN BE WORKED IN STRAIGHT LINES TO MAKE STRIPES, OR AS A DECORATIVE BORDER FOR THE HEM OF A SKIRT OR PANTS, OR ALONG THE EDGE OF A PILLOW.

STEP 1: Work the stitches along a real or imaginary line. Secure your thread on the back side of the fabric using a double knot (see page 46) and come up at A. Pull the thread through. Insert your needle down into the fabric at B, off to the side of your stitching line, and make a scooping stitch to bring it to the front at C on the stitching line. Make sure the thread is looped around the needle when you pull the needle through. Carefully pull the thread all the way through to form a loop that looks like a hook, as shown in the inset detail for Step 1.

STEP 2: To make the second feather stitch, insert the needle into the fabric at D on the other side of your stitching line, and make a scooping stitch to bring it to the front at E on the stitching line. The inset detail for Step 2 shows two feather stitches completed.

STEP 3: To make the third feather stitch, insert the needle into the fabric at F, on the same side of the stitching line as the first stitch, and make a scooping stitch to bring it to the front at G on the stitching line. The inset detail for Step 3 shows three feather stitches completed.

STEP 4: Continue stitching until you have worked all the feather stitches you want, remembering to always come up to the front of the fabric along the stitching line, and to alternate stitches on each side of the line. To finish, insert your needle down into the fabric at the bottom of the last hook and take a small stitch to anchor it. Finish by weaving the thread under the stitches on the back side as shown on page 70. Trim the end, leaving a 1/4" tail.

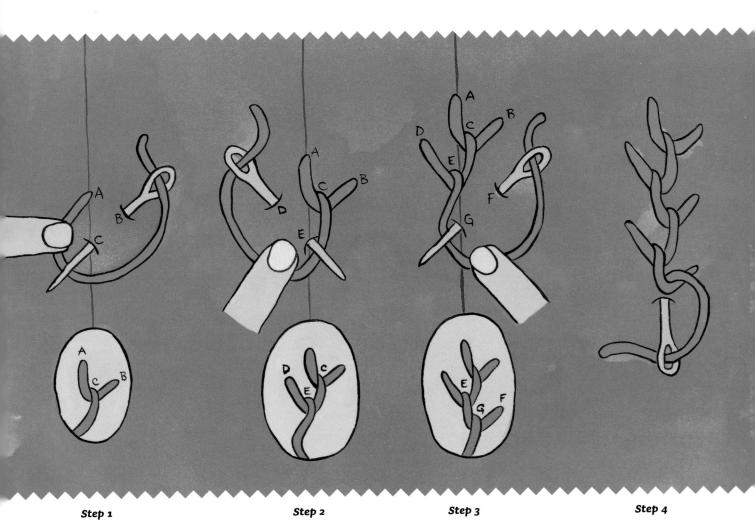

Step 1   **Step 2**   **Step 3**   **Step 4**

blanket stitch *scarf*

MAKE ANY SCARF—homemade or purchased—unique with a quick round of blanket stitch along the edges. When choosing fabric for this project, look for something thick and warm that is tightly woven so the edges won't fray. The length of your scarf depends on the width of the fabric, so it should be at least 50" wide.

The directions call for Persian wool, but you can also use wool handknitting yarn (as long as it's not too thick to thread through your needle) or cotton embroidery floss. Mix and match fabrics and yarns to find the combinations you like best.

1) *prepare the scarf*

Some fabrics have narrow bands along the edges that are more tightly woven and less flexible than the rest of the material; this part of the fabric is called a selvage. If your piece of scarf fabric has selvages, carefully trim them off. If you are using a piece of fabric that is not felted, and you can see the

---

Materials

1 (12-INCH) PIECE WOOL, MOHAIR, OR OTHER SUITABLE FABRIC AT LEAST 50" WIDE *(length of the scarf depends on the width of the fabric; the most common width you will find in fabric stores is 54" wide)*

2 (8-YARD) SKEINS PERSIAN WOOL, IN A COLOR TO CONTRAST WITH YOUR FABRIC

SIZE 16 CHENILLE NEEDLE

FABRIC SCISSORS

EMBROIDERY SCISSORS

RULER OR TAPE MEASURE

YARDSTICK

WATER-SOLUBLE MARKER OR DRESSMAKER'S MARKING CHALK, IN A COLOR THAT WILL SHOW ON YOUR FABRIC

THICK TOWELS OR BLANKET, FOR BLOCKING

---

blanket stitch

One of a Kind!
Mix and match fabrics
and yarns to make every
scarf you stitch unique.

individual threads, find the straight grain of the fabric as shown on page 10, and trim your fabric straight along all four sides.

Pick one side of the fabric to be the wrong side of the scarf. You will place all your knots and ends of yarn on this side. Using a ruler or yardstick and your marker, draw a line $1/2$" in from the edge, all the way around 4 sides of the fabric on the right side (the side you want to show). Mark a small dot every $1/2$" along this line; these dots are where you will insert your needle to embroider each blanket stitch. As you are making the dots, you can place them slightly closer together, or a little farther apart as you reach each corner, so that there is a dot in each corner that is $1/2$" away from both edges.

2 prepare the yarn

Separate two 2-ply strands of Persian wool about 32" long, following the instructions on page 14. You will stitch using two strands of thread.

3 embroider the scarf

Begin embroidering a few inches away from one corner. Secure your thread on the back side of the fabric with a double knot (see page 46) and bring the needle to the front very close to the edge. Continue working blanket stitch along the edge as shown on page 93 around all 4 sides of the scarf. Finish by taking the thread to the back side at the corner of the last stitch, and make a stitched knot (see page 46). Trim the end of the thread to about $1/4$" long. Start and end new threads as needed until you have finished all the embroidery. Each new strand should come to the front very close to the edge, but inside the curve of the last loop from the old thread, so the stitching looks continuous.

4 finish the scarf

Spray lightly or dab the sewing lines with water to remove all traces of the water-soluble marker. Place a pair of thick bath towels or a folded blanket on a flat surface like a table or mattress in an area where you can let your embroidery dry undisturbed. Lay the scarf out face up, and spray it with water so that it is damp all over. With your hands, gently pull the fabric straight, smooth, and flat. If necessary, place straight pins along the edges to hold it in place, and allow it to dry completely.

lazy daisy tote bags

THESE ROOMY TOTE BAGS are great fun to make and to carry around. Choose a strong fabric that your embroidery needle will pass through easily (the fabric has to be strong so it won't rip when you put your stuff in the bag). Or, buy a bag at the store and skip right to the embroidery instructions (Step 5).

1 prepare the fabric

With an adult's help, press the fabric with an iron so it lies flat. Find the straight grain of the fabric, and straighten the one cut end (see page 10).

Refer to the cutting layout for the tote bag on page 104 for cutting out your fabric pieces. Using a water-soluble marker and beginning at the straightened cut end, draw a rectangle 4" high and 36" wide. Draw a second rectangle 4" high by 36" wide right next to the first rectangle, so they share one long edge. These pieces will become your two handles. Draw a third rectangle 15" high and 30" wide for the bag. With your fabric scissors, cut out all three pieces. Using a ruler or yardstick and your marker, draw a sewing line 1/2" in from the edge, all the way around four sides of the fabric for the body of the bag.

Materials

3/4-YARD STRONG, SOLID-COLORED FABRIC, SUCH AS HEAVY COTTON OR WOOL, ABOUT 45" WIDE

1 (27-YARD) SKEIN SIZE 5 PEARL COTTON EMBROIDERY THREAD

SIZE 22 CHENILLE NEEDLE

SEWING THREAD TO MATCH BAG FABRIC

SEWING NEEDLE

FABRIC SCISSORS

EMBROIDERY SCISSORS

RULER OR YARDSTICK

WATER-SOLUBLE MARKER IN A COLOR THAT WILL SHOW ON YOUR FABRIC

PINS

IRON (optional)

running stitch · lazy daisy · backstitch

Tote-ally Cool!

The bags shown here were made with an assortment of different fabrics: an old wool blanket, linen from the fabric store, and cotton picked up at a thrift shop.

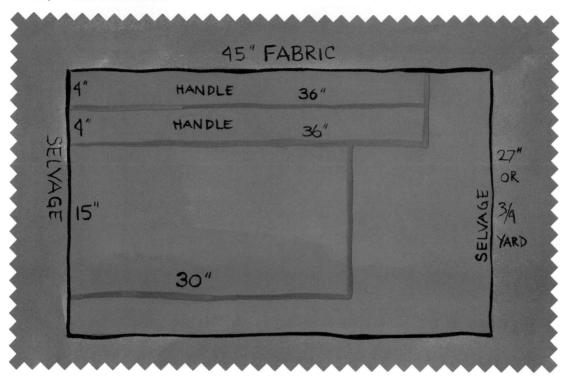

2 assemble the bag

With right sides of fabric facing each other, fold the bag piece in half so that the two short 15" sides meet, as shown in the top illustration at right. The fold will become the bottom of the bag. Pin the sides of the bag together. Thread the sewing needle with sewing thread and make a double knot in the end of the thread (see page 46). Begin stitching at the fold and sew the seams with running stitches about $^1/_8$" long and $^1/_8$"

apart, $^1/_2$" in from the edge. When you reach the other end of each seam, finish by taking the thread to the back and making a stitched knot (see page 46). Trim ends to $^1/_4$".

Fold under the raw edges at the top of the bag $^1/_2$". Press the fold and the seams with an iron so it lies flat. Fold the edge under $^1/_2$" one more time to enclose the raw edge, and press again. Pin the folded edge all the way around the opening as shown in the bottom illustration at right. Remove the pearl cotton thread from the skein as

Step 2 *Fold and Pin the Bag*

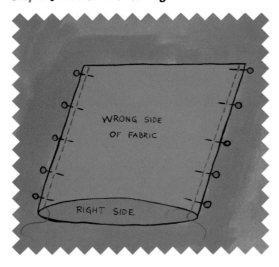

Step 2 *Pin, Press, and Sew Top of Bag*

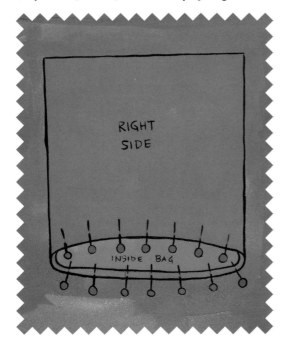

shown on page 14. Thread the chenille needle with the pearl cotton and make a double knot in the end. With the right side of the bag facing you, sew close to the fold line all the way around with backstitches (see page 57) about ¼" long.

3) make the handles

Fold one of the handle pieces in half so that it measures 2" wide and 36" long. Press the fold so it lies flat. Open up the handle flat again, and fold each raw edge into the center fold line you just created and press each side. Fold again along the first fold line and press. Your handle will now measure 1" wide and 36" long. Repeat for the other handle. Thread the chenille needle with the pearl cotton and make a double knot in the end of the thread. Sew the open edge shut with running stitches about ¼" long placed ¼" from the edge.

4) attach handles

With your ruler, measure in 3" from each seam on both sides of the bag and place a mark with a water-soluble marker on the inside surface of the bag. These 4 points are where you will attach the bag handles.

Lay the bag flat on the table with the opening at the top. Pin one end of a handle to a mark on the inside of the bag, with about ¹/₂" of the handle extending past the line of stitching inside the bag. Pin the other end of the handle to the matching mark on the other side. The illustration above shows the bag with all four ends of the handles pinned in place.

Thread the chenille needle with the pearl cotton and make a double knot in the end of the thread. Attach the handle with backstitches ¹/₄" long, stitching exactly over your original line of stitching around the top of the bag. Repeat for the other handle.

⑤ embroider the lazy daisies

With your water-soluble marker, mark the position of 7 or 8 flower centers on each side of the bag. Make sure the flower centers are far enough apart so the flowers won't touch each other. Thread the chenille needle with the pearl cotton and make a double knot in the end of the thread. Begin stitching by coming to the front for the first flower, and work lazy daisy stitches (see page 95) to form flower petals around each center mark. To end, make a small stitch to anchor the bottom of the last loop (as shown in Figure 3 on page 95). Make a stitched knot on the back of the fabric to end the thread for this flower. Trim the end to ¹/₄". Starting and ending a separate strand for each daisy (so there won't be any long strands on the back of the bag to snag when you fill it), repeat for the remaining flowers. Spray lightly or dab the stitching lines with water to remove all traces of the water-soluble marker.

Why Not?

You can stitch just about anything on these tote bags. Instead of lazy daisies, try curlicues in chain stitch, starbursts in straight stitch, a big monogram in stem stitch, or whatever else you can think up.

curlicue doll **pillow** & feather-stitch **Quilt**

THIS PROJECT WAS DESIGNED for a doll but can, of course, work for a person as well. The curlicue pillow looks great on beds and sofas. The feather-stitch quilt can be made larger for a real bed but that is, of course, a lot of work.

If you don't want to sew your own pillow and quilt, you can embroider on store-bought items. Using a water-soluble marker, draw the curlicues on a pillowcase and work chain stitch over them. To create stitching lines for a store-bought blanket, draw two straight lines down its length using a water-soluble marker and yardstick, then work feather stitch over the lines.

chain stitch · running stitch
feather stitch · whipstitch

Materials

curlicue doll pillow

$^1/_4$-YARD SOLID-COLOR COTTON FABRIC, AT LEAST 36" WIDE

1 (27-YARD) SKEIN SIZE 5 PEARL COTTON EMBROIDERY THREAD

MATCHING SEWING THREAD, FOR ASSEMBLING THE PILLOW

SIZE 3 EMBROIDERY NEEDLE

SEWING NEEDLE

FABRIC SCISSORS

EMBROIDERY SCISSORS

POLYESTER FIBERFILL STUFFING, ENOUGH TO FILL YOUR PILLOW

RULER OR YARDSTICK

WATER-SOLUBLE MARKER IN A COLOR THAT WILL SHOW ON YOUR FABRIC

EMBROIDERY HOOP *(optional)*

PINS

IRON *(optional)*

Materials

feather-stitch quilt

$^2/_3$-YARD MEDIUM-COLORED COTTON FABRIC,
    AT LEAST 36" WIDE

$^1/_3$-YARD DARK-COLORED COTTON FABRIC,
    AT LEAST 36" WIDE

$^7/_8$-YARD LIGHT-COLORED LINING FABRIC,
    COTTON OR SYNTHETIC, AT LEAST 36" WIDE

1 (27-YARD) SKEIN SIZE 5 PEARL COTTON
    EMBROIDERY THREAD

SEWING THREAD TO MATCH ONE OF THE
    QUILT FABRIC COLORS

SIZE 22 CHENILLE NEEDLE

SEWING NEEDLE

FABRIC SCISSORS

EMBROIDERY SCISSORS

RULER OR YARDSTICK

WATER-SOLUBLE MARKER OR DRESSMAKER'S
    CHALK IN A COLOR THAT WILL SHOW
    ON YOUR FABRIC

EMBROIDERY HOOP *(optional)*

PINS

IRON *(optional)*

curlicue doll pillow

1 prepare the pillow fabric

Find the straight grain on the fabric along one long cut side (see page 10). Using the ruler and water-soluble marker, draw 2 rectangles on the fabric, each 14" wide and 8" high. With your fabric scissors, cut out both rectangles. On one piece, use a water-soluble marker to draw a line $^1/2$" in from the edge around all four sides—this will be your sewing line when you are ready to sew both pieces of the pillow together after you have finished the embroidery.

2 draw curlicues on pillow

With a water-soluble marker, draw nine curlicues in different sizes all over the marked piece of fabric. To make the pillow more interesting, make curlicues in different directions and sizes. If you don't like how your curlicues look, spray lightly or dab the lines with water to remove them. Wait for the fabric to dry before drawing the curlicues again because the water-soluble marker will not work on wet fabric. You can use a hair dryer to speed up the process.

3 embroider the curlicues

If desired, place the first section of the fabric to be embroidered in an embroidery hoop (see page 48).

Remove the pearl cotton thread from the skein as shown on page 14. Thread the needle and make a double knot in the end of the thread (see page 46). Begin stitching by coming to the front at the outside end of one of the curlicues, and work chain stitch (see page 94) along the line using stitches about $^1/8$" long. When you reach the other end of the curlicue, take the thread to the back side and weave in the ends as shown on page 70. Trim the end to $^1/4$". Repeat until all of the curlicues are embroidered.

4 assemble the pillow

Lay your embroidered piece flat on a table with the right side of the embroidery (the side without the knots) facing you. Place the piece of fabric without any embroidery on top. Using straight pins, pin the two pieces together around all four sides. Thread a 36" length of sewing thread and make a double knot in the end. With the sewing thread, sew the two pieces together using a small running stitch (see page 55) about $^1/8$" long and following the stitching line you drew $^1/2$"

in from the edge, leaving a 5" opening in the middle of one side for stuffing.

When you have finished sewing the seam, trim the point off each corner, as shown on page 47. This will remove the excess fabric from inside the corner so your pillow points will be neat and sharp. Turn the pillow right side out through the hole you left in the seam so that the embroidered side is facing you. Use something with a rounded point, like the eraser end of a pencil, to push out the points from the inside, being careful not to poke through the fabric. With an adult's help, press the pillow with an iron to neaten it. Stuff the pillow with fiberfill. To close the pillow opening, fold the raw fabric to the inside of the pillow along the seam line. Pin the opening shut. Using whipstitch, sew the opening of the pillow closed using stitches about $^1/4$" long, as shown for the Simple Cross-Stitch Pillow on page 49. Spray lightly or dab the stitching lines with water to remove all traces of the water-soluble marker.

feather-stitch quilt

1 prepare the quilt fabric

Find the straight grain on one long cut side of both fabric pieces and trim the fabric (see

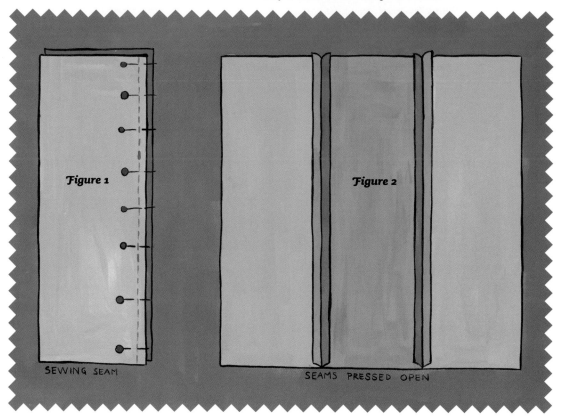

Figure 1

SEWING SEAM

Figure 2

SEAMS PRESSED OPEN

page 10). Using the ruler and water-soluble marker or dressmaker's chalk, draw 2 rectangles on the medium cotton fabric, each 11" wide and 28" long. With your fabric scissors, cut out both rectangles. Draw a rectangle on the dark cotton fabric, 11" wide and 28" long, and cut out this rectangle. On all 3 pieces, draw a line ¹/₂" in from the edge around all 4 sides—this is the line you will use to assemble the quilt.

2 *assemble the quilt panels*

Place one medium and the dark piece of fabric together and pin them along a long side, as shown in Figure 1 above. Thread a 36" length of sewing thread and make a double knot (see page 46) in the end of the thread. With the sewing thread, sew the two pieces together using a small running stitch (see page 55) about ¹/₈" long and following the stitching line you drew ¹/₂" in from the edge. Remove the pins as you work.

Pin the remaining medium piece of fabric to the other long side of the dark fabric, and seam them together. You will now have a striped piece of fabric with one color in the center and two matching colors on either side. With an adult's help, press the seams open with an iron on the back side of the quilt so they lie flat against their own color fabric, as shown in Figure 2 at left.

③ embroider the quilt top

You will be embroidering a line of feather stitches on top of each of the two seams of the quilt top. Think of the seam as the imaginary line described with the feather stitch instructions on page 96.

If desired, place the first section of the fabric to be embroidered in an embroidery hoop (see page 48).

Remove the pearl cotton thread from the skein as shown on page 14. Thread the needle and make a double knot in the end of the thread. Begin stitching by coming to the front at the end of one seam, and work feather stitch along the seam line using stitches about ¹/₂" tall and extending out about ¹/₄" to each side. When you reach the other end of the seam, end the thread with

a stitched knot (see page 46). Trim the end to ¹/₄". Repeat for the second seam.

④ prepare and attach the lining

Place the quilt, embroidery side down, on the lining fabric with two sides even. Pin the quilt top and the lining together along all 4 outside edges. Carefully cut the lining fabric on the remaining two sides so that it is the same size as the quilt. Thread a 36" length of sewing thread and make a double knot in the end of the thread. With the sewing thread, sew the two pieces together using a small running stitch about ¹/₈" long and following the stitching line you drew ¹/₂" in from the edge on the quilt top. Leave a 5" opening in the middle of one side for turning quilt right side out.

When you have finished sewing the seam, trim the points off the corners, turn the quilt right side out, press, and close the opening, following the second paragraph of Step 4 of the pillow instructions.

Embroidery Samplers

Needlework samplers have been made for hundreds of years. The tradition began in Europe, where the earliest known sampler is dated 1502. Historically, samplers were made by young girls and women as learning pieces for trying out new stitches. (Of course, now both boys and girls can stitch samplers if they want to.) The embroiderers passed ideas, stitches, and new patterns on to friends and family by showing and sharing their samplers among themselves. This sharing of ideas is how different stitches traveled from one community to another.

When the first colonists came to America, they brought this sampler-making tradition with them. When a girl began learning needlework, her first sampler was usually the alphabet and numbers worked in cross-stitch, and she began stitching at about the same age that she learned to read and write. By making an alphabet sampler, a girl learned to stitch, count threads, and to concentrate.

Most American samplers had a border on the sides and across the top made of leaves and vines, flowers, or geometric patterns. Sometimes a poem, phrase, or passage from the Bible was included. Often, at the bottom of the sampler, there was a scene with a house, barn, trees, farm animals, family, wildlife, and flowers. Most of the time, the sampler-maker stitched her name, birthday, and year the sampler was made. Some samplers even listed all the members of the family with the dates of important family events, like births, deaths, and weddings—a perfect way to make a visual diary of the family at a time when there were no photographs.

You can make your own sampler. To make it look traditional, find some tan-colored linen to stitch on and several colors of embroidery floss. Draw a geometric or floral border around the sides and across the top of the fabric. Draw a picture of your house, your family, and animals. Add your name, birthday, and the year you make the sampler. Work the pictures in any combination of stitches you like. You will be carrying on an age-old tradition.

slumber-party
pillowcases

THIS MULTIMEDIA PROJECT combines fabric printing with embroidery to make a cheerful polka-dotted pillowcase. The polka dots are stamped onto the fabric with a cork dipped in paint; then, after the paint has dried, the dots are edged in chain stitch. This is a great project for a slumber party— or any party, really. Kids who are new to embroidery only have to learn one stitch— chain stitch—and everyone goes home with a very special souvenir. Just be sure all the pillowcases are washed and dried before the party starts.

(1) prepare work surface and pillowcase for stamping

Cover the work surface with a drop cloth. Slip the paper bag inside the prewashed pillowcase to keep paint from the stamped side of the pillowcase from seeping through to the other side. Lay the pillowcase out flat on the work surface.

Materials

1 (100% COTTON) PILLOWCASE, WASHED
    AND DRIED
2 SKEINS EMBROIDERY FLOSS
SIZE 5 EMBROIDERY NEEDLE
EMBROIDERY SCISSORS
1 (1-OUNCE) SQUEEZE BOTTLE NONTOXIC
    FABRIC PAINT, AVAILABLE AT CRAFT STORES
WATER-SOLUBLE MARKER IN A COLOR THAT
    WILL SHOW ON YOUR FABRIC (optional)
PAPER BAG, ABOUT THE SAME SIZE AS
    THE PILLOWCASE
DROP CLOTH
ONE CORK WITH AN END ABOUT $^3/_4$" ACROSS
    FOR STAMPING, AVAILABLE AT CRAFT
    AND HARDWARE STORES
SMALL PAPER PLATE, FOR STAMPING
PAINTBRUSH
IRON (optional)

chain stitch

116

For an extra festive pillowcase, stamp your polka dots in several different colors of fabric paint and embroider around the dots in different colors of floss.

on the paint bottle, usually about an hour. If you can't wait, speed up the process by using a hair dryer. If you want polka dots on both sides of your pillowcase, repeat this step on the second side.

(3) embroider the polka dots

Cut a 30" length of floss. Separate out 4 of the 6 strands as shown on page 15; you will be stitching with 4 strands for this project. Thread the needle and make a double knot in the end of the thread (see page 46). Begin stitching by coming to the front on the edge of the first polka dot, and make a line of chain stitches about $^1/8$" long around the dot. To end, take a small stitch to anchor the bottom of the last loop (see page 94). Weave the ends through the back of the stitches as shown on page 70. Trim the end to $^1/4$". Repeat for the remaining polka dots, starting and ending a separate thread for each polka dot so there won't be any long strands to catch on the back.

(2) stamp the polka dots

If you like, use a water-soluble marker to mark where you want your dots to be. Squeeze a small amount of fabric paint — about the size of a quarter — onto the paper plate. Using a paintbrush, pick up some of the paint and dab it on one end of the cork. To practice stamping, press the cork onto a piece of scrap fabric or paper. When you are happy with how your polka dots look, begin stamping them on one side of the pillowcase. Let the pillowcase dry thoroughly, according to the directions

Hosting an Embroidery Party

NOW THAT YOU KNOW HOW MUCH FUN IT IS TO EMBROIDER, DON'T YOU WANT TO SHARE IT WITH YOUR FRIENDS? GO AHEAD AND PLAN A PARTY.

1 make invitations

For the cover of each invitation, embroider a simple design on a small piece of fabric and glue it on neatly. Inside, write something like this:

Please come to my house to learn embroidery!
Date
Time
Your Name and Address
Bring 6 different colors of embroidery
*   floss to share.*
I hope you can come!

2 pick a project

Select something you think most of your friends would like to make that can be completed in the time you've allowed for the party. You can apply the stitches from any of the projects in this book to a small project like a felt bookmark. Make a list of the supplies you will need (aside from the embroidery floss, which your friends will be bringing). Visit your local needlework or craft store to purchase the supplies.

3 make a sample

Make up a sample project so everyone can see what they are making before they get started.

Have fun!

Fancy
Stitches

So far, most of the stitches you have learned
have been easy to do and only take one or two steps to
complete, but a needle and thread can be made to do
many more neat tricks. All the fancy stitches in this
chapter are made by wrapping the thread around a needle
(French and bullion knots), or wrapping the thread around
another stitch (spider web and woven bars).
These stitches are raised above the surface of the
fabric to add texture. Fancy stitches are often worked
in combination with more basic stitches.

There are hundreds of fancy stitches you can learn.
To explore them, go to your local library or craft
or needlework store and take a look at the stitch
dictionaries they have on their shelves.

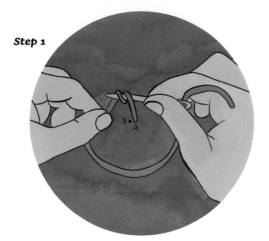

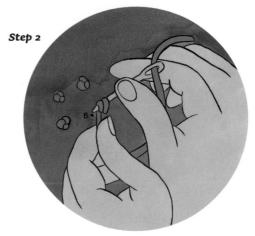

French Knots

FRENCH KNOTS LEND THEMSELVES TO ALL KINDS OF DECORATION——THE MOST COMMON USE IS IN THE MIDDLE OF A LAZY DAISY TO MARK THE CENTER OF THE FLOWER. FRENCH KNOTS ALSO MAKE PERFECT GRAPES AND CURLY HAIR. YOU CAN EVEN USE THEM AS POLKA DOTS ALL OVER A PILLOW, OR IN LINES AS A BORDER. OFTEN FRENCH KNOTS ARE WORKED SEPARATELY, STARTING AND ENDING THE THREAD FOR EACH KNOT. THIS IS USEFUL IF YOU ARE WORKING ON A THIN, SEE-THROUGH FABRIC WHERE THREADS CONNECTING ONE FRENCH KNOT TO ANOTHER MIGHT SHOW THROUGH ON THE

STEP 1: Secure your thread on the back side of the fabric with a double knot (see page 46) and come up at A. Pull the thread through. With a finger and thumb from your hand that is not holding the needle, pinch the thread about 1/2" away from A, and wrap the thread around the needle in either direction twice.

STEP 2: Pulling gently on the thread the whole time to hold the wraps snugly against the needle, rotate the point of the needle

down toward the fabric and insert it next to A at B. (If you put the needle in the exact same hole at A, the knot will disappear through to the back.) Still holding the thread tight so the wraps stay against the needle, push the needle to the back of the fabric and pull through. A small knot will appear on the surface. To finish, turn the fabric over so you can see the back side. Right behind the French knot (so it won't show on the front), make a stitched knot (see page 46). Trim the thread to 1/4".

Bullion Knot

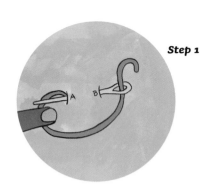

Step 1

THE BULLION KNOT STITCH IS SOMETIMES CALLED THE CATERPILLAR STITCH BECAUSE IT LOOKS LIKE A CATERPILLAR.

STEP 1: Secure your thread on the back side of the fabric with a double knot (see page 46) and come up at A. Pull the thread through. Insert the needle at B, where you want the knot to end, and make a scooping stitch to bring it to the front at A again. Do not pull the needle all the way through, but leave about 1" of the needle sticking out of the fabric.

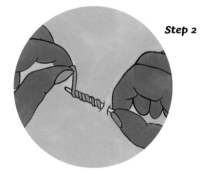

Step 2

STEP 2: With a finger and thumb from your hand that is not holding the needle, pinch the thread about 2" away from A, and wrap the thread around the needle about seven times in the direction shown in the illustration. If you wrap the wrong way, the plies of the thread will start to untwist and loosen.

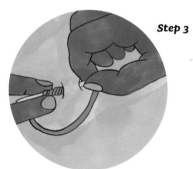

Step 3

STEP 3: Holding the wraps snugly against the needle, gently push the needle all the way through the tunnel of the wraps, as is about to happen in the illustration. The needle will disappear into the fabric so you can't push any more. Now grab the point with the other hand, and begin pulling the needle out while pushing the wraps snugly toward the eye end of the needle. Tighten the knot, and adjust the wraps with your fingers or the point of your needle so they lie flat and even.

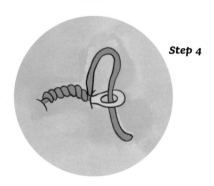

Step 4

STEP 4: To finish, insert the needle at B again and pull the thread through to the back. Turn the fabric over to the back side and, right behind the bullion knot (so it won't show on front), make a stitched knot (see page 46). Trim the end of the thread to $1/4$".

Step 1   **Step 2**

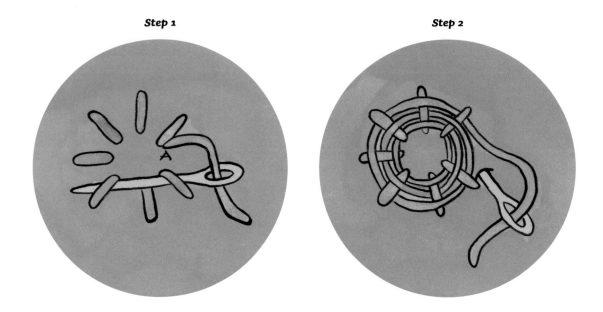

Spider Web Stitch

THE SPIDER WEB STITCH BEGINS WITH THE STRAIGHT STITCH SHOWN ON PAGE 60. THE RAYS ARE THEN WOVEN TO FORM THE WEB.

STEP 1: Secure your thread on the back side of the fabric with a double knot (see page 46) and come up at A. Make a sunburst shape about 2" across with seven 1" spokes, and a 1" hole in the center (if necessary, refer to the straight stitch directions on page 60). When the spokes are finished, bring your needle to the front again at A.

STEP 2: Use the needle to weave over and under the spokes around and around in a circle until the spider web is filled in as much as you like. Be careful not to pull the thread too tight so the web lays nice and flat. To finish, insert your needle down into the fabric very close to the end of one of the spokes and take the thread to the back. Make a stitched knot (see page 46). Trim the end, leaving a $^1/_4$" tail.

Woven Bar Stitch *(or Needle Weaving)*

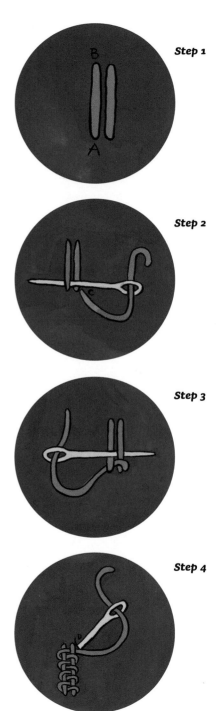

Step 1

Step 2

Step 3

Step 4

THE WOVEN BAR STITCH IS SIMILAR TO THE SPIDER WEB STITCH, BUT INSTEAD OF WEAVING AROUND IN A CIRCLE YOU WEAVE BACK AND FORTH OVER TWO STRAIGHT STITCHES. THIS MAKES A LITTLE PIECE OF THIN WOVEN FABRIC THAT SEEMS TO FLOAT ON THE SURFACE OF THE EMBROIDERY. YOU CAN USE IT FOR LEAVES, PETALS, AND CLOTHING ON LITTLE PEOPLE. ONCE YOU GET THE HANG OF THIS STITCH, YOU CAN INCREASE THE NUMBER OF STRAIGHT STITCHES YOU BEGIN WITH TO MAKE LARGER WOVEN BARS.

STEP 1: Secure your thread on the back side of the fabric with a double knot (see page 46) and come up at A. Pull the thread all the way through, then insert the needle at B, about 1" away from A. Repeat to make a second stitch the same length, very close to the first stitch, but not using the same holes in the fabric.

STEP 2: Bring the needle to the front at C. Begin weaving by going over the first thread and under the second thread.

STEP 3: Turn the needle to point in the opposite direction, and again go over the first thread and under the second thread. Continue until the straight stitch threads are completely covered.

STEP 4: When you are happy with the way the woven bar looks, insert the needle to the back of the fabric at D, very close to the end of one of the straight stitches. Make a stitched knot (see page 46) and trim the end, leaving a ¼" tail.

one world *medallions*

THESE MEDALLIONS ARE GREAT for practicing different types of embroidery stitches. Use them to decorate all sorts of cool stuff, such as bags, barrettes, hats, pants, a journal, cards, backpacks, walls, windows, or Christmas trees. The motifs come from different cultures and have been used by embroiderers for thousands of years. Isn't it neat to imagine a person living long ago in a faraway place wearing an outfit with the very same motif that's on your baseball cap or barrette?

(1) transfer the design

Choose a motif from the ones shown on page 142 and enlarge it to the size you want on a copy machine (the motifs shown at right were enlarged between 115% and 150%). Transfer the motif to the felt according to the instructions on page 71, using dressmaker's tracing paper. If the transfer markings aren't dark enough on the fabric, use the water-soluble marker to draw on top of them. Or draw your own design with a water-soluble marker. Make sure you leave 1/4" to 1/2" blank around the motif on all sides.

Materials

SEVERAL PIECES OF FELT, IN DIFFERENT COLORS

SMALL AMOUNTS OF PERSIAN WOOL OR
    EMBROIDERY FLOSS IN SEVERAL
    DIFFERENT COLORS

SIZE 22 CHENILLE NEEDLE, OR ANY
    SHARP-POINTED EMBROIDERY NEEDLE
    WITH AN EYE THAT WILL FIT YOUR THREAD

FABRIC SCISSORS

EMBROIDERY SCISSORS

RULER OR TAPE MEASURE

WATER-SOLUBLE FABRIC MARKER OR
    DRESSMAKER'S TRACING PAPER IN A COLOR
    THAT WILL SHOW ON YOUR FELT

PINS

ASSORTED SCRAPS OF RIBBON, RICKRACK,
    OR SEAM BINDING (6" TO 8" LONG), FOR
    MAKING HANGING MEDALLIONS (*optional*)

FABRIC GLUE

IRON (*optional*)

All stitches — the sky is the limit!

Bright Idea!
If you don't want to
make a felt medallion,
you can embroider any
of these designs directly
on other surfaces like
blue jeans, pillows, or
T-shirts (with permission
from Mom and Dad,
of course).

(2) cut the felt

Using fabric scissors, cut around the motif, being careful to leave a margin of at least $1/4$" to $1/2$" around the embroidery lines on all sides. You can cut any shape you like — a circle, oval, square, rectangle, diamond, or hexagon. Use your motif as your guide to the finished shape. To make cutting out the shapes easier, trace common household objects as guides, like the bottom of a glass, a coaster, or a pack of cards.

(3) choose stitches and colors

It's not necessary to plan out your whole design before you start; in fact it's often easier and more fun to choose the stitches and colors as you go. To get you started, refer to the Stitch Guide at right. Separate the strands of your embroidery thread according to the directions on page 14. Experiment using different numbers of strands to create different effects. The samples shown here were made with 1 strand of Persian wool or 4 strands of embroidery floss. Work the stitches you've chosen as instructed in the different chapters.

MEDALLION STITCH GUIDE

Following are some suggestions for where to use different stitches. But remember, you are the boss when it comes to your embroidery, and if you like the way your embroidery looks with the stitches you are using, then you are doing it right.

Thin, Straight, or Curved Lines *stem stitch, backstitch, chain stitch*

Short Lines *single straight stitches*

Zigzag Lines *feather stitch, backstitch, running stitch*

Filling in Solid Shapes With One Color *satin stitch, or work stem or chain stitches very closely together to make a solid area of color*

Small Dots and Circles *French knots, satin stitch, spider web stitch*

Small Ovals *bullion knots, satin stitch, woven bar stitch*

Rectangles *woven bar stitch, satin stitch*

Flowers *straight stitch, spider web stitch, lazy daisy stitch*

Leaves *satin stitch, single chain stitches (one part of a lazy daisy), woven bar stitch*

4 *finish the medallion*

Spray lightly or dab the sewing lines with water to remove all traces of the water-soluble marker, or brush away any remaining dressmaker's tracing paper lines. To even out your stitches and make your medallions look neat and nice, you can block them, as follows: Place a thick bath towel on a flat surface like a table or mattress in an area where you can let your embroidery dry undisturbed. Lay the medallions on the towel face up, and spray with water so that they are damp all over. With your hands, gently pull the felt straight, smooth, and flat. If necessary, pin the medallions to the towel along the edges to hold them in place.

Above: Here's a flower shown on a medallion on page 127 recreated on a pair of blue jeans. To see more embroidery on the front of these jeans, turn to page 133.

Right: Nicholas and Claude think the medallions on their baseball caps are fun.

About Motifs

A motif is a single small drawing or image that can be a design all by itself, or can make up part of a larger design. Geometric shapes like circles, squares, and triangles are very simple motifs. A flower composed of center, petals, and stem is a more complicated motif. In embroidery, you can make up your own motifs or copy ones that you see in other places, such as on books, wallpaper, rugs, or fabric. Some motifs are used by many different cultures throughout the world, and some are unique to a specific culture. Here's a list of some of the traditional motifs shown on the One World Medallions, with explanations of what they've come to symbolize.

Circles

A symbol for the sun, which represents life, warmth, and the never-ending cycle of life because the sun rises and sets every day.

Trees

A symbol for birth, life, and death. A common motif called the Tree of Life shows birds, animals, fruits, and flowers.

Flowers and Fruit

A symbol of the bounty of the harvest and the importance of the earth as a source of growing things.

Curves or Crescent Shapes

A curved symbol can stand for animals with horns, like deer and cows. A crescent can also represent the moon. Two curves turned inward to face each other become a heart, the symbol of love.

Crosses

A cross made with both lines the same length, like a plus sign, can symbolize stars and the heavens.

If you leave enough open space around your embroidered motif you'll have room to frame it with other stitches, such as running stitch (as shown on this backpack).

(5) attach medallion to object

To attach the medallion to an object, such as a barrette, baseball cap, or backpack, squeeze a small amount of fabric glue onto the back of the medallion, and spread it carefully out to the edges. Try not to use too much glue or it will be messy and come through to the front side of the embroidery. Press the medallion onto the object and lay it flat to dry. If attaching the medallion to a rounded object, like a barrette, hold the medallion in place for a few minutes so that the glue will attach securely at all points.

(6) make a hanging ornament

To make felt medallions into ornaments, cut a piece of ribbon, rickrack, or seam binding about 6" to 8" long. Fold it in half and use fabric glue to attach it to the back side of the medallion. Make sure you glue the ribbon to the top point of the design so that it will hang with the top side up.

Making It Yours:
Embroidering on Your Clothing

ONCE YOU KNOW A FEW EMBROIDERY STITCHES, YOU CAN EASILY PERSONALIZE YOUR BLUE JEANS, BACKPACKS, T-SHIRTS, SHIRTS, DRESSES, PILLOWS, AND MORE. HERE ARE SOME EASY IDEAS TO GET YOU STARTED:

On a T-shirt

Add a row of lazy daisy flowers, French knots, or bullion knots around the neckline or embroider your monogram on the front with stem or outline stitch.

On hems, collars, pockets, or any opening of any piece of clothing

Embroider a row or two of running stitch in one or more colors or add a row of blanket stitch in a contrasting color to make a neat edge.

On blue jeans

The sky is the limit! Decorate the pockets, hems, and knees. When you're embroidering on denim, you may need to use a metal thimble to push the needle through the fabric; if not, you may hurt your finger by pushing hard.

On backpacks or canvas bags

Add your name or monogram to the side of a bag; place a row of decorative stitching around the top edge; or decorate the handles with lines of chain or feather stitches. You may need a thimble for this also.

About Tess's Jeans

Tess loves butterflies. To decorate her jeans, first she drew a butterfly with a few simple lines on a piece of paper. Then she transferred the design to her jeans using dressmaker's tracing paper, and went over the lines again with a water-soluble marker to make them darker. Then she embroidered the butterfly using satin stitch, French knots, and other stitches in bright colors that showed up well against the blue denim.

Finally, she added some curved stems in backstitch, and topped each stem with a different-colored lazy daisy. She entered her jeans in the county fair and won a blue ribbon!

tea party

THIS FANCIFUL TEA-PARTY SET —tea cozy, place mats, and napkin rings—was made from one old twin-size blanket cut into four pieces and dyed four different colors (bright green, teal, orange, and cobalt blue).

tea cozy

1 enlarge the tea cozy pattern

Take the pattern shown on page 137 to a copy center and enlarge it to 240% its size. The enlarged pattern will fit on an 11" x 17" piece of paper. If you like, you can draw your own design instead of using the one shown here. Just be sure that your design will fit on the piece of felt.

2 prepare the tea cozy yarn

Separate two 2-ply strands of Persian wool about 32" long, following the instructions on page 14. You will stitch using two strands of thread.

Materials

tea cozy

ONE 12-INCH PIECE VERY HEAVY WOOL FABRIC (often called coating fabric) OR FELT AT LEAST 45" WIDE

7 (8-YARD) SKEINS PERSIAN WOOL, IN 5 DIFFERENT COLORS

1/3-YARD PIECE BUCKRAM AT LEAST 45" WIDE (optional, for stiffening the cozy)

place mats (to make six place mats)

3 (18-INCH) PIECES VERY HEAVY WOOL FABRIC OR FELT AT LEAST 45" WIDE; ONE PIECE EACH OF 3 DIFFERENT COLORS

6 (8-YARD) SKEINS PERSIAN WOOL, 2 SKEINS EACH IN 3 DIFFERENT COLORS

napkin rings

1 (7-INCH) PIECE VERY HEAVY WOOL FABRIC OR FELT AT LEAST 45" WIDE; OR USE SCRAPS LEFTOVER FROM TEA COZY AND PLACE MATS

5 (8-YARD) SKEINS PERSIAN WOOL, ONE EACH IN 5 DIFFERENT COLORS; OR LEFTOVERS FROM TEA COZY AND PLACE MATS

* For a list of the stitches used in this project, see Stitch Guide on page 136.

bringing the needle to the front very close to the edge. Work blanket stitch along the edge as shown on page 93.

Finish by taking the thread to the back side at the corner of the last stitch, and make a stitched knot (see page 46). Trim the end of the thread to about $1/4$" long. Embroider blanket stitch in the same way along the bottom edge on the plain side of the tea cozy.

7) assemble the tea cozy

Using a water-soluble marker, draw a line around the rounded edge of the tea cozy $1/4$" in from the edge. Mark dots along this line every $3/8$". Pin the two pieces of the tea cozy together with the right sides (the sides you want to show) on the outside. Work blanket stitch around the edge through both layers of fabric.

8) block the tea cozy

Spray lightly or dab the sewing lines with water to remove all traces of the water-soluble marker. Place a pair of thick bath towels on a flat surface like a table or mattress in an area where you can let your embroidery dry undisturbed. Lay cozy out with the main embroidered side up, and spray with water so that it is damp all over. With your hands, gently pull the fabric

straight, smooth, and flat. If necessary, place straight pins along the edges to hold them in place. Allow the cozy to dry completely.

9) stiffen the tea cozy *(optional)*

Using your fabric scissors, cut two pieces of buckram about $1/2$" smaller than the tea cozy all the way around. Slip the pieces inside the cozy and attach one to each side in several places with small dots of fabric glue. Do not use too much glue or it may seep through to the outside. Trim the buckram again if any of it shows on the outside.

place mats

1) prepare place mat fabric and yarn

Prepare fabric as necessary (see steps 2 and 3 of tea cozy instructions). Draw two rectangles on each piece of fabric using a water-soluble marker, each 12" high and 18" wide. Cut out all 6 rectangles using fabric scissors. Pick one side of the fabric to be the wrong side of the place mat. You will place all your knots and ends of yarn on this side. Using a ruler or yardstick and your marker, draw a line $3/8$" in from the edge, all the way around 4 sides of the fabric on the right side (the side you want to show). Mark a small dot every $1/2$" along this line; these

Party Time!

Getting together with friends is extra-special when you set the table with your own handiwork.

dots are where you will insert your needle to embroider each stitch. As you are making the dots, you can place them slightly closer together, or a little farther apart, as you reach each corner, so that there is a dot in each corner that is $1/2$" away from both edges.

3 embroider the placemats

Begin embroidering 2" to 3" away from one corner. Secure your thread on the back side of the fabric with a double knot (see page 46), bringing the needle to the front very close to the edge. Work blanket stitch along the edge around all 4 sides of the place mat.

End by taking the thread to the back side at the corner of the last stitch, and make a stitched knot (see page 46). Trim the end of the thread to about $1/4$" long.

4 block the placemats

Block place mats following Step 8 of tea cozy instructions.

napkin rings

1 prepare napkin ring fabric

Prepare fabric as necessary. See Step 3 of tea cozy instructions. Draw rectangles 2 $1/2$" high by 6 $1/2$" wide on the fabric, making sure you follow the straight grain, if it is visible. Draw and cut one rectangle for each napkin ring.

3 embroider napkin rings

Fold the 2 short sides of the napkin rings together and mark the fold with a water-soluble marker to indicate the center of the rectangle. Open the rectangle and draw a large circle about 1 $1/2$" in diameter in the center of the fabric. Draw a smaller circle about $1/2$" in diameter inside the larger circle. Using one 2-ply strand of Persian wool, work a 9-point sunburst within the circles following straight-stitch instructions on page 60. With a second color, work a spider web on top of the sunburst (see page 124.)

4 assemble napkin rings

Overlap the short ends of the napkin rings by 1" and pin closed. Using running stitch (see page 55) and a single strand of Persian wool, sew across the double layer of fabric to close the ring.

Block, following Step 8 of tea cozy instructions.

Templates

Personal Pincushion (page 66)

Felt Journal Cover (page 86)

Old-Fashioned Cat (page 72)

Old-Fashioned Dog (page 72)

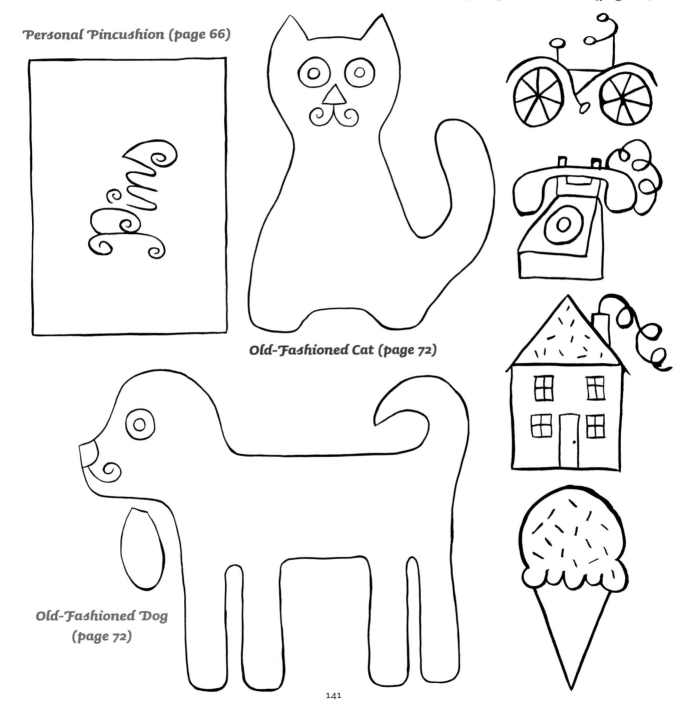

One World Medallions
(page 126)

Acknowledgments

Many people contributed their talent to *Kids' Embroidery*. John Gruen took the beautiful photos, with the assistance of Chris King and stylist James Leland Day. My editor and friend, Melanie Falick, organized my ideas and imparted her vision and style. Publisher Leslie Stoker believed that kids would love to learn to stitch. Lori Gayle, technical editor extraordinaire, brought sense and order to my words. Graphic designer Jennifer Wagner pulled everything together into this lovely package.

Laura Timmerman, librarian of the small but powerful Robertson Memorial Library, found all the books I requested and organized the Monday morning stitchery class. Thanks to all the great kids and their moms for coming. Your enthusiasm for stitching fueled my creativity and your laughter was contagious.

For stitching projects shown in the photos, I am grateful to Peggy Brown and her "girl scouts," Sarah Brown-Anson, Jeanne Bartlett, Rachel Becker, Ali Post, and Tess Vreeland; Nancy Nicholas (my mom), Laurie Nicholas Rabe and Nancy Belletete (my sisters); Olivia Rabe and Celia, Camille, and Lillian Belletete (my nieces); plus my friends Kay Dougherty, Cathy Payson, and Elizabeth Smith. Celia Belletete also supplied her artwork for me to embellish on page 80.

Thanks to all of the models (and to their parents for letting them participate): Elita Baker, Jeanne Bartlett, Rachel Becker, Celia, Camille, and Lillian Belletete, Vishakha Bellizia-Lyons, Sarah Brown-Anson, Nicholas Duprey (my nephew), Isabelle and Eliza Granahan-Field, Claude, Zachary, and Matthew Jean, Olivia Rabe, Amie and Kellie Schiller, and Tess Vreeland. For helping me find the kids, thanks to Kristin Damon, Nicole Cusano, and Beth Weissman.

Kay and Mike Dougherty of Seven South Bakery made the colorful cupcakes on page 139 and sustained us during the photo shoot with pig cookies. Susan Mills and Alan Getz of JCA encouraged me and supplied me with their fabulous wool. All of the companies that contributed supplies for the projects are listed at right.

And thank you to Mark, my husband, and Julia, our daughter, who supported and entertained me, and most of all, lived through the creative chaos.

Sources for Supplies

Paternayan Persian wool
JCA
35 Scales La.
Townsend, MA 01469
508.597.8794

cotton embroidery floss and pearl cotton
DMC
10 Port Kearny
South Kearny, NJ 07032
973.589.0606

wool felt
Magic Cabin Dolls
PO Box 1049
Madison, VA 22727
888.623.6557
www.magiccabin.com

Morehouse Farm
141 Milan Hill Rd.
Milan, NY 12571
845.758.6493

wool and cotton dyes
Dharma Trading Co.
PO Box 150916
San Rafael, CA 94915
800.542.5227

fabric paint
Duncan Enterprises
5673 E. Shields Ave.
Fresno, CA 93727
559.291.4444

Index